"Keeping things simple, as we o
has unlocked the way to make si
and living. Through equally fasc
Simplicity Playbook for Innovato
that change the world and appea

ROB FINDLAY
Digital Innovation Lead, Amazon ٠٠cυ ɔervices
Founder of Next Money

"A must-read for anyone who wants to venture into design thinking.
The references in this book are tried-and-tested concepts that work!"

WYSON LIM
Head of Group Wealth Management, OCBC Bank

"Jin is both engaging and insightful. Her commitment to a structured
yet user-centric approach towards simple and elegant solutions to
workplace challenges and industry transformation needs will continue to inspire others, especially those who wish to be change agents
and facilitators of innovation teams."

DR LIM LAI CHENG
Executive Director, Singapore Management University Academy

"Jin Kang Møller is a simplicity guru. She got me started on my simplicity journey, and it changed the trajectory of my career significantly. I came to realise, from Jin's teachings and modelling, that
simplicity is the heart, mind and soul of good experience. In this
book, Jin transcends theory, giving the reader practical guidance on
making complex customer experiences and communications more
simple. I highly recommend the book for any business leader who
recognises the obvious – simpler is better – and needs a playbook for
achieving that noble goal."

MARK MCCORMICK
SVP, Strategic Design, Innovation Group, Wells Fargo

"In *The Simplicity Playbook for Innovators*, Jin Kang Møller breaks
down innovation into simple, easy-to-understand concepts and
shows how less is more when creating something new. This book is
especially relevant in today's post-Covid-19 world, where we need
to be agile and creative in coping with the many unprecedented
challenges."

DENNIS TAN
CEO, Prudential Singapore

The Simplicity Playbook for Innovators

Creating lovable experiences
in a complicated world

JIN KANG MØLLER

Marshall Cavendish
Business

Published in 2020 by Marshall Cavendish Business
An imprint of Marshall Cavendish International

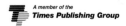

A member of the
Times Publishing Group

Other Marshall Cavendish Offices:
Marshall Cavendish Corporation, 800 Westchester Ave, Suite N-641, Rye Brook, NY 10573, USA • Marshall Cavendish International (Thailand) Co Ltd, 253 Asoke, 16th Floor, Sukhumvit 21 Road, Klongtoey Nua, Wattana, Bangkok 10110, Thailand • Marshall Cavendish (Malaysia) Sdn Bhd, Times Subang, Lot 46, Subang Hi-Tech Industrial Park, Batu Tiga, 40000 Shah Alam, Selangor Darul Ehsan, Malaysia

Marshall Cavendish is a registered trademark of Times Publishing Limited

National Library Board, Singapore Cataloguing in Publication Data

Name(s): Møller, Jin Kang.
Title: The Simplicity Playbook for Innovators : Creating lovable experiences in a complicated world / Jin Kang Møller.
Description: Singapore : Marshall Cavendish Business, [2020]
Identifier(s): OCN 1165405577 | ISBN 978-981-4893-26-8 (paperback)
Subject(s): LCSH: Organizational change. | Simplicity. | Creative thinking.
Classification: DDC 658.406–dc23

Printed in Singapore

For Sabina, Ben and Noah,
who make my life nothing but simple,
but simply beautiful

For Jonas,
who always anchors me back to simplicity

Contents

Introduction

Any intelligent fool can make things bigger and more complex. It takes a touch of genius and a lot of courage to move in the opposite direction.
— Ernst F. Schumacher

My quest for simplicity started in 2008, when the Global Financial Crisis hit the industry.

The bankruptcy of Lehman Brothers was a seminal moment in the Global Financial Crisis. The world saw the deepest economic recession since the Great Depression in the 1930s. At that time, I was working with Credit Suisse's private banking division as a customer experience designer. I witnessed how this crisis affected the financial lives of millions of people and saw how their trust in financial institutions and the industry plummeted. One of the reasons behind this crisis were the so-called "innovative products". They were devised with very sophisticated mechanisms that leveraged many different financial instruments. The "innovation" reached a level that was too complicated for ordinary customers.

The crisis taught the industry that pursing innovation without considering customers' point of view is dangerous; it damages businesses and destroys customers' trust. It was a painful wake-up call. As a direct response to this crisis, *simplifying the customer experience* became imperative for restoring and advancing the industry. It became my mission and passion.

Fast forward to 2020, and "innovation" has become the new buzzword.

Spurred by advancements in Fintech, Blockchain and AI, the financial industry, along with other industries, has been undergoing a massive wave of change. This environment presents endless opportunities for disruption, with many emerging players now having the capacity to substitute financial services businesses. The lines between industries are blurring, and it has become critical to build a creative business model that goes beyond traditional industry lines in order to succeed.

However, as companies race to explore opportunities for innovation, I can't help but feel that **customer-centricity has lost its importance.** In companies' meeting rooms these days, I hear more about the latest technologies, emerging players or building ecosystems, and less about the needs and pain points of real people, the customers. It reminds me of the climate and circumstances that culminated in the 2008 financial crisis, and I ask myself: Where does the pursuit of innovation without customers' point of view lead us?

On 11 March 2020, as I entered the final stages of writing this book, the WHO declared Covid-19 a pandemic. The toll that it is taking on lives and businesses is immense, and even experts can't predict how long it will continue, or agree on the best way to manage it. The world we operate in now is truly very complicated, and companies face greater challenges than ever.

It is time to regain our focus.

One thing is certain: This crisis will give us clarity on what really matters to our customers and to our businesses today. After the 2008 crisis, financial services companies shifted towards "customer-centricity" and took tangible steps to simplify customer experiences. This shift created a strong foundation for the next wave of change: digital banking. Today, the companies that will come out stronger from the pandemic are the ones that can shake off irrelevant practices and forge towards the new formula for success.

The change is already happening. Going through months-long lockdowns, people have become more conscious about what's essential in life. Companies that previously baulked at the notion of working from home are now driven to leverage on technology to emulate and even enhance the face-to-face working experience. Retail players – even local market vendors – are embracing this crisis as an opportunity to reinvent themselves to engage with consumers in new ways.

More than ever, companies need to transform their value proposition with creativity and agility. However, change in this time of uncertainty can be exceptionally difficult to navigate, and companies need a North Star to guide them into the future.

I find the answer in Simplicity.

What does simplicity mean in the era of the innovation imperative?

Simplicity is the quality of being easy to understand or do, as the dictionary defines it. But the effect of simplicity is beyond being easy. It is about the essentials, knowing what matters most and reducing the rest. It is also state of mind – a feeling of calmness, focus, confidence.

I therefore define simplicity as **an experience that makes things easy for users and leaves a positive emotional effect.** And simplicity as an experience needs to be deliberately designed.

Simplicity is key to any kind of innovation – whether it's digital transformation or service innovation.

Innovation succeeds when we're able to change people's behaviour, whether it's changing customers' behaviour to adopt our products or services, or employees' behaviour to operationalise a new way of creating value. **By making it simple for your target users, you increase their ability to change their behaviour.**

Think about how Facebook or Instagram have become part of our daily habits. These digital platforms make sharing our life moments and connecting with people so easy and enjoyable. Their simplicity of operation has changed our behaviour.

Designing a positive user experience is crucial in building a platform business to drive change among consumers, service providers and partners. Think about how Airbnb or Uber have successfully brought millions of people together and empowered them to interact with each other to offer and buy services. There is no way such shifts in business model can happen unless the user experience is intuitive and provides emotional assurance.

Simplicity needs to be cultivated.

We often hear "Less is more". People intuitively appreciate simplicity. However, when it comes to applying simplicity in the business context, companies seem to lack deliberate action and methods. Achieving simplicity requires strong leadership as well as awareness, discipline and hard work by individuals in the team.

Successful simplification work is the outcome of an obsessive customer-centric approach, relentless challenging of the status quo, and commitment to stripping off complexity layer by layer, some of which have accumulated over a long period of time.

Contrary to common belief, simplicity is in everyone's power. It does not belong only to visionaries or creative geniuses. I have seen sparks in people when the methods for simplicity are taught to them and they realise that achieving simplicity is actually doable even for non-creatives. When the awareness and sensitivity for simplicity is coupled with this new-found confidence, it can drive a powerful and long-lasting change in the way organisations make decisions and innovate.

This playbook is about "how" – and it has been tested.

Drawing on my 20 years of experience as a practitioner, I have identified the principles and methods that result in the biggest impact for achieving simplicity. This playbook is designed to accompany you throughout your innovation journey – from understanding how simplicity helps you innovate better, to ways in which you can use simplicity to make an impact, change organisational culture and sustain these changes.

In Part I, I will lay the foundation by establishing the connection between simplicity and innovation. In Part II, I introduce the principles of simplification using a framework I designed called the Simplicity Diamond. The diamond consists of five principles that transform the way you look at five business practice areas:

- **How to run effective customer research:** Get fuelled by empathy (Chapter 3)

- **How to mobilise people:** Dance with complexity (Chapter 4)

- **How to craft a simple value proposition:** Focus (Chapter 5)

- **How to simplify communications:** Speak human (Chapter 6)

- **How design customer experiences:** Design lovable experiences (Chapter 7)

In each facet of the Simplicity Diamond, you will find practical tools which have been applied and tested, particularly in legacy companies dealing with complex processes and systems. Finally, in Part III, we will discuss how you can drive change and make it happen. Every innovation endeavour is essentially about change management – influencing people and changing culture.

I feel optimistic because this pandemic crisis will drive creativity and transformation. I saw how the financial industry came out stronger after 2008. And having seen how successful simplicity has been as a North Star to help companies navigate the challenges in times of uncertainty, I'm confident of its effectiveness.

With this playbook, I hope to empower you with both the awareness and the methods to uncover what really matters for your business, and to design new experiences that your customers simply love.

Part I
Why simplicity

Making the simple complicated is commonplace.
Making the complicated simple... that's creativity.
 — Charles Mingus

Chapter 1
Simplicity leads to innovation

Simplify or innovate?

After the 2008 financial crisis, one of the questions I often got asked in companies' meeting rooms was this:

> "When should we 'innovate', when should we 'simplify'?"

The question came to me rather as a surprise the first time. I'd never thought about this opposition of simplicity versus innovation before. I've since observed that many people do seem to think of simplicity as "improving the existing", as opposed to innovation, which is perceived as "looking for the new".

On another occasion, the CEO of a private bank asked me this question:

> "Where should I allocate my resources? To 'innovation', or to 'simplifying the existing'?"

Having to strike a balance between improving the old and looking for the new seems to be a constant challenge in today's fast-changing and uncertain environment.

But is simplicity really at odds with innovation?

While leading a broad range of strategic customer experience initiatives, I discovered that there is a direct connection between simplicity and innovation. In fact, more often than not, **innovation happened as a result of pursuing simplicity.**

In our teams, we never started with the mindset of "Let's innovate". Instead, we were always deeply concerned with simplicity – making the current experience simple and enjoyable. We identified what mattered most to customers and removed frictions through a rigorous design process. We ended up delivering successful innovation as the result of designing experiences to be simple. Because people loved the experiences we designed.

Innovation takes the form of simple customer experiences.

That innovation is the result of simplification is not my observation alone. People deeply engaged in the work of simplicity have pointed out the powerful connection between innovation and simplicity. Alan Siegel and Irene Etzkorn, leading voices of simplicity and the authors of a remarkable book, *Simple*, express the connection perfectly:

> "The most powerful forms of innovation don't manifest themselves in new bells and whistles. They take the form of better customer experiences. And one of the best ways to improve any experience is to simplify it – to remove complications, unnecessary layers, hassles and distraction while focusing in on the essence of what people want and need in the particular situation."[1]

When I spoke to Mark McCormick, Senior Vice President at Wells Fargo and a passionate practitioner of simplicity, he explained how, in financial services, the greatest innovators are those organisations that have focused on simplifying a key banking task, such as getting a mortgage, refinancing a student loan, or doing a quick transfer of money from person to person. Innovation, for Mark, is hollow unless it's in service to simplicity. People talk about "innovation", but they really mean simplification.[2]

Defining simplicity in the era of the innovation imperative

When we Google "simplicity", we get a glimpse of how people perceive it.

We see images of things or scenes that are natural, minimal or "Zen", and objects that perform essential functions and exhibit certain design aesthetics.

The Cambridge English Dictionary defines simplicity as *the quality of being easy to understand or do*. But the effect of simplicity is beyond being easy. We feel simplicity in life when we have a picnic in the meadow on a sunny spring day. Or when we drink a freshly brewed coffee on a Sunday morning. **We "feel" simplicity when we are satisfied with a few things that matter to us**. The feeling can be joy, calmness or happiness. In fact, the word "simplicity" doesn't seem to have synonyms; rather, it's a combination of many things. Perhaps simplicity is something we experience, just like having an intuition or a feeling.

Simplicity is an experience.

Inspired by the moments of simplicity in life, in the business context I define simplicity as this:

> Simplicity is an experience that makes things easy for users and leaves positive emotions.

In other words, simplicity is about usability (easy to use), as well as pleasure (feels good). Simplifying the complex is only half the equation. The pleasure part – creating positive emotions in customers – is just as crucial in designing for simplicity.

If we can learn to approach simplicity as an experience, rather than as an abstract concept, we'll be able to see what experiences need to be simplified and what emotions need to be created – and deliberately design for them. The emotions you seek to create are determined by your brand values or your project objectives. For example, for a financial services company, the emotion they want to leave their customers with might be "feeling confident".

A story of the little black dress

A great example of how simplicity is an experience is the "little black dress" designed by Coco Chanel in 1926.[3] She observed that women at the time had to go through a rather painful process when "decorating" themselves. To meet the social norms of being sophisticated, they had to wear layers of dresses, tight corsets, accessories and heavy hats with feathers or even actual fruits on

them! It took hours for women to get dressed, and wearing these layers of garments certainly wasn't comfortable.

Coco Chanel's observation of oppressive fashion in the late 19th century gave her a bold design concept: defining the new elegance through simplifying. The little black dress was designed to eliminate the pains associated with female finery. She shortened the length of the dress and removed extraneous ornaments. Jersey was introduced as a fabric – which was used for men's undergarments at that time – to make the dress light and stretchy.

In today's terms, Coco Chanel was clearly a user-centric designer. Her design process started with empathy for her target customers. She designed for her users, to simplify their daily ritual of getting dressed. The little black dress was easy to wear, yet made women feel comfortable, elegant and trendy. They were hooked!

We humans desire simplicity. And this is more true than ever in today's world of overload – the overload of information, features and choices. People welcome solutions that simplify and enhance their lives. The most powerful innovation takes the form of simplicity.

How simplicity leads to innovation

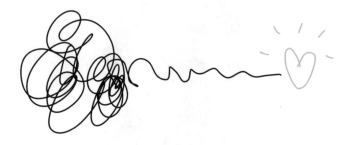

People are intrinsically drawn to simpler products and services because they save time and effort. At the same time, simplicity plays a key role in making innovation successful for two reasons:

1. Simplicity increases people's ability to change.

2. Simplicity creates visible impact.

1. Simplicity increases people's ability to change.

Digital technology drives constant change in the way companies create value. New business models are created, and the way we as consumers buy and use products or services has changed fundamentally. Banks used to be a place we go, but banking has now become a service that we can do anytime, anywhere. Platform businesses like Uber, Grab or Airbnb, which bring together parties that supply services (e.g. accommodation) and parties that need such services (guests), have changed how businesses create value in an unprecedented way.

This shift in business model is built upon simplicity as a foundation. There is no way consumers can carry out banking activities by themselves unless the user experience is simple. Platform businesses won't work unless the user experience is infused with simplicity and a sense of trust for both parties.

Innovation happens only when people's behaviour changes. By making things simpler for users, companies can create the desired behavioural change, such as adopting a new product or a new way of doing things. Think about how Instagram has become a habit for many of us. The creators of such digital platforms have made sharing and connecting so easy and enjoyable that we change our behaviour to make greater use of it.

The behaviour change is also about a company's employees. In order to implement new processes or strategies, the key to success lies in making things easy for employees to achieve the desired behaviour. So simplicity is a great strategy for companies to entice customers, as well as employees, because it increases people's ability to change their behaviour.

Simplifying a form to achieve desired behaviour

Take a look at the financial needs analysis forms on the next page. Originally, it took an average of 40 minutes to complete. When I observed the people who used this form – both bank advisors and customers – I could see that the complicatedness of the form wasn't helping any of them get their jobs done.

The advisors were reluctant to use the form upfront to understand their customers' financial needs (which was the form's

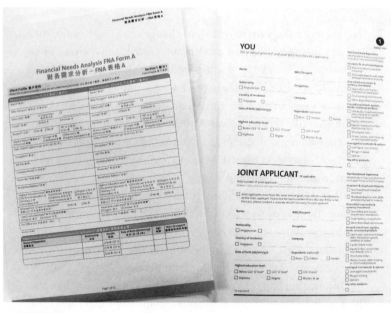

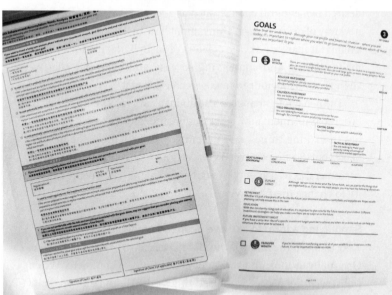

Financial needs analysis form:
Before (left) and after (right)

intention); instead they preferred to use it only towards the end of the meeting, merely to fulfil the process requirements.

For customers, having to fill out the complex form was a turn-off. Some customers requested not to proceed with the meeting the moment the form was placed on the table, as it looked like it was going to take a long time to complete.

So we looked at simplifying this form, to make it a friendly conversation tool instead of a roadblock. We redesigned it from scratch and reduced the total number of pages, with the result that the average time it took to fill out the form was shortened from 40 minutes to 5–10 minutes.

And the behaviour of the users changed completely! The bank advisors started naturally using this form in the early stages of discussion, both as a stimulus for conversation and to fulfil the compliance requirements. Customers who used the new form were more engaged in discussing financial matters, without feeling they were just filling out a form.

Once we simplified this paper form, the work needed to digitise this process and to design the interface was smooth – because the paper form was already designed with the user experience in mind, with an intuitive flow that would achieve the desired behaviour.

Making it simple is the only way to engage with today's users

Dr B.J. Fogg, a professor at Stanford University, explains the relationship between simplicity and behavioural change.[4] In order to perform a target behaviour, a person must have the ability to do so. If the person's ability is lacking, there are two paths to increasing it.

Firstly, you can train people to improve their skills, to perform the target behaviour. This, however, is the hard path. How many people have time and patience to read a user manual or the FAQ? People expect things to just work.

The second path is through simplicity. When companies learn to simplify their processes and interfaces, they will be able to nudge people towards the target behaviour. Simplicity thus becomes the very foundation of innovation.

2. Simplicity creates impact.

The impact of simplicity is visible and often immediate – in the form of revenue increase, market share or customer loyalty. Whether it is simplifying a complex form, a product or an entire experience, these innovations produce remarkable results.

Simplicity sells

When OCBC Bank simplified one of their fund product brochures, there was a 150% increase in sales after just a month. The product itself hadn't changed; we had just simplified communication.

When we went on to simplify more complex products – such as a life insurance offering – we made an even greater impact. Typically, buying an insurance product involves a lot of documents to read, and many forms to fill. Some insurance products require a medical examination and an underwriting process. The more complex the product and the larger the coverage amount, the longer the process takes and the more specialists are involved.

This time, the work of simplification spanned all touchpoints and across broader processes. Starting with making the brochures and forms easier to understand, we went on to simplify the sales, application and underwriting processes. For example, the way the sales people work with the product experts was streamlined to provide a better customer experience when introducing the product. The underwriting process, which involves broader stakeholders to evaluate the risk and exposures of the potential customer, was shortened from an average of 4 weeks to less than a week. With the entire experience simplified, we saw an amazing result: an eightfold increase in contract values.

The "World's Simplest Brands" report[5] confirms that simple brands are those that put clarity and ease at the heart of the customer experience. The study found that 55% of consumers are willing to pay more for simpler experiences, and 64% of consumers are likely to recommend a brand because it provides simpler experiences and communication. Simplicity inspires trust and strengthens loyalty.

Simplicity leads to business innovation

Richard Koch and Greg Lockwood are successful investors and consultants who have spent their lives researching and scrutinising businesses to invest in. They argue that simplifying is the golden thread that connects and explains nearly every market disrupter in history. By focusing on investing in so-called "simplifiers", Koch reportedly grew his wealth from $214 million to $373 million within the span of two years.

In their book, *Simplify: How the Best Businesses in the World Succeed* (2016), Koch and Lockwood identify two strategies for simplification.[6]

Price simplifying requires cutting the price of a product or service in half or more. Contrary to common belief, Henry Ford didn't invent the automobile. At the time, there were other automobile manufacturers, who were producing expensive cars mostly for well-to-do people. What made Ford's business successful was the massive price reduction achieved through his innovation process and the standardising of materials. When Ford brought down the price of his cars by 75%, his sales went up – not by 75%, but 70,000%.

Proposition simplifying involves creating a product that is useful, easy to use and aesthetically pleasing. For example, Microsoft Windows as an operating system is useful, but fairly complicated. Apple's iPad on the other hand, is very easy and joyful to use. Even a small child can immediately operate it and enjoy using it.

The authors' strategies deeply resonate with my observation of how simplicity is indeed the key to innovation, in particular the strategy of proposition simplifying.

Simplicity is an experience that is made easy for users, and that creates a positive emotion. Simplicity matters because it drives behavioural change, which is fundamental in all innovation. In today's digital world, competitive advantage lies in creating simple experiences, for this allows companies to demand a price premium.

Chapter 2
Simplicity is everyone's job

Whose job is it to achieve simplicity?

To achieve simplicity, we need strong leadership.

Leaders in an organisation must want simplicity as a priority, and take the responsibility for making it happen. Because more often than not, simplification requires challenging the status quo.

Steve Jobs was undeniably one of the most charismatic leaders who believed in the power of simplicity. He would reject his team's designs and prototypes if they in any way failed to distil an idea to its essence. The expression "Steve hit us with the Simple Stick" became common inside Apple, encapsulating the value of simplicity as the core constant in driving innovation. This ethos, which started in Steve Jobs' mind, is of course now burned deep into the company's DNA.[1]

In my simplicity journey at OCBC Bank, the strong leadership that provided the conditions for driving change was the Chief Operating Officer, Ching Wei Hong, who was internally feared and revered, just like Steve Jobs at Apple. He was the one who had the exceptional vision and neverending energy to create a great experience for the bank's customers. Under his leadership, everything the bank produced and all its processes were challenged through the lens of simplicity.

Another of my champions was the Head of Global Wealth Management, Wyson Lim, who believed in the value of simplicity and embraced the journey wholeheartedly even though the design methods I introduced were quite new at the time. Tan Siew Lee, Head of Wealth Management, got her hands dirty with co-creation and prototyping (which will be introduced in Chapter 4). Owing to her hands-on leadership, the department has become the champion of building simplicity as a capability.

Empower everyone to tackle day-to-day complexity.

Organisations, just like any living organism, are bound to evolve to become more complex over time. Unless companies build a sustainable mechanism that confronts this intrinsic complexity and constantly shed the excess, simplicity won't be achieved.

It is crucial, therefore, to empower everyone in an organisation to tackle day-to-day complexity. Having a dedicated team of specialists (or hiring consultants) might be a great starting point, but it won't be sustainable unless your organisation cultivates its own capabilities.

During my Simplicity Bootcamp with managers and executives, I've seen the spark in their eyes when the methods for simplicity are taught to them, and they realise that achieving simplicity is actually doable. Very often, the biggest sparks come from the so-called IT folks or legal professionals, who are often considered to be the internal bottlenecks on the simplicity journey. When I offer them a new lens and new tools, they become the most enthusiastic ones, and come up with many great ideas to achieve simplicity.

The Simplicity Diamond

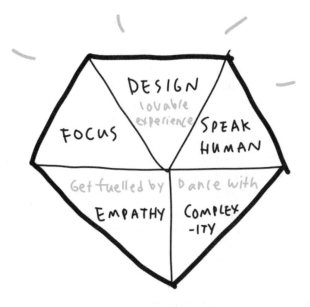

In my 20 years of experience as a design practitioner, I have led, participated in, and witnessed many digital transformation journeys – each with its unique challenges and approaches. There are many ideas out there. Some sound good in theory, but may not work in the real, messy world of innovation. Some take many years to bear fruit; others work immediately, with results that last.

The most important thing I've learnt is that while adopting a new method matters, **what drives real change is people – the alignment and energy of a group working together.** It's about developing a mindset of simplicity in individuals who care deeply about customers, who are passionate about doing the right thing, who love trying new ideas.

Getting to this stage means learning how to internalise the principles that matter. Looking at the projects I've worked on over the years, I can see that there are five key principles that have resulted in the biggest impact, which I have brought together in a framework I call the Simplicity Diamond.

We are told that a diamond is forever, and simplicity is just as timeless. And like a diamond, simplicity is valued for clarity. When people are empowered to internalise and implement the principles of simplicity in their daily work, your business can create more value for its customers, and for itself.

Overview of the 5 principles

The five key principles are arranged in the five facets of a diamond. The two at the bottom are foundational principles related to research and internal working models, which are crucial for building the culture of the organisation. The three at the top are likely visible to customers, as the outcomes of applying these principles will be reflected in product development, communications and customer experience design.

For each principle, I will be showing you (a) the **strategic shift** and (b) the **methods** for implementing simplicity as strategy. In Part II of the book we will delve into each principle in detail, but here is an overview:

---

1 Get fuelled by empathy

The shift: Data → **Insight**

Empathy is about putting yourself in your customers' shoes. It is an incredibly powerful tool, because there is a direct connection between the ability to empathise and to reframe business problems. Use empathy as your strategic asset to turn mere data into insight. By shifting your mindset from gathering data to crafting powerful insights, you'll uncover a wealth of innovation opportunities.

The methods: Research methods to maximise empathy; involving stakeholders in the research process; Experience Labs; synthesising and reframing.

---

2 Dance with complexity

The shift: Manage processes → **Mobilise people**

Complexity doesn't have to be the bottleneck on your road to simplicity. In fact, the more complexity your business has, the greater the opportunities for creating a breakthrough innovation! By shifting your perspective away from the typical process-oriented approach to a people-centric approach, you can unlock people's creativity to solve the most complex problems.

The methods: Layers of complexity; change management; concretising the abstract; divergent and convergent thinking; co-creation; prototyping; visualising complexity.

3 Focus

The shift: More → **Less but better**

Attention is one of the most valuable resources of the digital age. As our business grows, we are tempted to create more products and add more features to attract more customers and increase the level of engagement. Instead, find your innovation opportunities in mindful reduction: doing fewer things, but better. When you offer focus, you show that you value your customers' time. In return, they put their trust in you.

The methods: Questions for focus; the Golden Circle; Jobs-to-be-done; the sweet spot; focus statements.

4 Speak human

The shift: Automate → **Humanise**

Conversational interfaces and voice-based interaction have become commonplace in communications between businesses and customers. In seeking to increase efficiency, we are often tempted to eliminate human elements through AI or digitalisation. However, we need to shift our mindset from automating processes to humanising the experience, to convey the simplicity and warmth of human interaction through any medium.

The methods: Ten Commandments of speaking human; using stories; bringing personality; humanising chatbots and legalese.

5 Design lovable experiences

The shift: Viable product → **Lovable experience**

Simplifying human experiences does not mean giving people the bare minimum. The goal of simplicity is to leave a positive emotion, whether it's love, joy or confidence. Go beyond making just a viable product to crafting lovable experiences. When customers love your product, the decision-making is simplified. Love creates long-lasting emotional connections with your customers.

The methods: Minimum Lovable Product; journey mapping; elements of experience design; aesthetics and sensorial experience; basics of visual design.

In the next five chapters, I will go into each of the five principles of the Simplicity Diamond and provide you with all the practical tools and real-life examples you will need to internalise them as yours.

Let's get started.

Part II
How to simplify

Chapter 3

Get fuelled by empathy

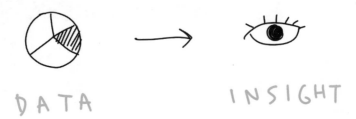

DATA → INSIGHT

Sell your cleverness and buy bewilderment.
Cleverness is mere opinion.
Bewilderment brings intuitive knowledge.
  — Rumi

IN 2010, I WAS TASKED with an exciting new mission: to conceptualise a new banking concept for millennials, which later launched as FRANK by OCBC.[1] The success of this project was critical as the bank faced a serious problem: low market share among young people aged between 16 and 29. We had to find a new way to capture and grow the future banking generation.

There was of course a wealth of data gathered by reputable consulting companies on how to attract millennials. Millennials are digital-savvy, they are the generation of entitlement, they are driven by purpose, the studies said. We could rationally understand these characteristics, but **we couldn't feel who these millennials really were.** We were determined to get out of the office and find out more about them by physically being with them and putting ourselves in their shoes.

The entire cross-functional project team took part. We hung out with millennials at malls, ate dinner with them, went shopping and even clubbing with them, and spent a lot of time looking in their wallets and talking about money.

From our efforts, we not only learned about these millennials' financial needs but also got to know them as people and understand their values and aspirations. We uncovered a trove of previously undocumented behaviours (as you'll see in the next section) that completely upended our notions of their attitudes to money, their expectations, their aspirations.

Inspired by these observations, stories and insights, we shaped the strategic direction of FRANK by OCBC, which positioned OCBC as the market leader in the segment.

What we were doing in this process was **gaining empathy, and using it to drive new insights and perspectives.** Empathy grows out of an experiential process of discovery. This means getting out of the office and talking to your customers instead of conducting a survey. This means observing how customers are solving their problems, rather than reading a study on consumer behaviour. People in the organisation must be given an environment where they can see, hear and feel the real experiences of their customers.

In this chapter, I will introduce empathy as the magic ingredient that fuels the search for simplicity. And we will discuss research methods to maximise empathy and craft powerful insights for innovation.

In this chapter

3.1 When we empathise, we gain new perspectives.
3.2 Make every research count.
3.3 Don't do research alone. Involve your stakeholders.
3.4 Be inspired by your customers, but distinguish between data and insight.
3.5 Synthesise to uncover insights.
3.6 Relentlessly pursue reframing.

When we empathise,
we gain new perspectives.

What is empathy?

Empathy is the ability to understand how other people think and feel, and the ability to see the world through their eyes.

We often think of empathy as a personal trait. We say someone is empathetic when they are able to take the perspective of another person and to recognise another person's emotions. Nurses are a good example of professionals who regularly need to exhibit empathy in dealing with patients.

Simplicity starts with empathy.

Simplicity lives in people's perceptions, not in what your company says. Simplicity is perceived and experienced. That's why simplification starts with having empathy, putting ourselves in customers' shoes to understand how they see, feel and do things.

In this diagram, the yellow circle represents the mental model we all have, which is based on our own experience or knowledge.

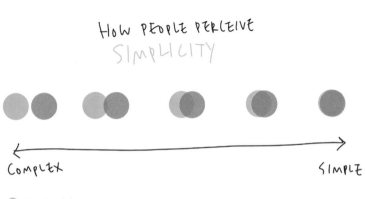

Mental model

Knowledge needed to understand

The grey circle represents the knowledge required to understand or perform something. When these two circles come closer together, people perceive something to be simple; when these two circles are further apart, people perceive that thing to be complex.

So the only strategy for simplification is to empathise with people and to get closer to their mental models. When we design something that is closer to people's existing mental models, they perceive it to be simple.

Empathy improves the ability to reframe.

Empathy is a choice that organisations can make to forge connections with customers. Empathy allow us to unlock new opportunities by connecting us with our customers at an emotional level, where we can better understand their circumstances and their deeper needs, which in turn opens up our perspectives. There is a direct link between empathy and the ability to reframe.

This is a compelling reason for putting in the time and effort to spend time with your customers – it pays off in your innovation endeavour. It's also probably much cheaper than commissioning custom research by a big consulting firm. Get out of the office and meet your customers and be inspired.

The story of FRANK by OCBC

Creating a new banking concept based on empathy

Throughout the initial stage of conceptualising FRANK by OCBC, the time that the team members spent in the shoes of millennials provided the solid foundation for constant inspiration and guidance. For a strategic initiative of this scale, there is always the risk that the vision may feel vague or complicated to achieve. Seeing customers as a source of inspiration was crucial for navigating through this innovation process.

Fresh perspectives in shaping the new banking experience

When we went out to spend time with millennials, we started noticing very interesting behaviours. For example, it emerged that shopping malls served as a social platform for many young people. They would meet at a mall, eat there, hang out there. To me, who was new to Singapore at the time, it was amazing to see how much social interaction was taking place in the malls. I could finally understand why people jokingly say shopping is the national sport in Singapore. Because it wasn't only about buying things. It was also a social activity and a way for people to express their style and personality in the vibrant multicultural city.

Another interesting discovery we made was this: One of the students we'd been following had a small sticky note pasted on the back of her ATM card. You can see what it looks like on the next page. Here, she would write down her expenditure – every item and its cost. She explained to us:

> "I get an allowance from my parents. I know they are working hard to support me during my studies. I want to make sure I don't overspend."

This incident surprised our team. It seemed to run counter to many of the studies we'd read. They may be labelled a generation of entitlement, but the young people in Singapore we met clearly had a deep sense of responsibility and respect towards their parents.

All these stories and observations fuelled us with a new burst of energy. We began to see our mission from a fresh perspective:

- While we had initially planned for the new banking concept to be fully digital, we started to recognise the importance of physical spaces like shopping malls among young people in Singapore.

- The idea emerged that millennials have a deep sense of control and desire to achieve their financial goals.

- Being style-conscious and wanting to express themselves was a distinct characteristic of the millennials we observed. Could we make a banking product a "fashion" item?

- How might we emulate the shopping experience in the new banking concept?

With this train of thought, we crafted the initial concept for FRANK: A simple, stylish and meaningful banking experience for millennials. We then immediately built a series of prototypes to make this concept tangible and testable. (Prototyping will be discussed in greater detail in Chapter 4.)

First, we prototyped the idea of a banking card becoming a fashion item:

Then we prototyped the "store", the physical space where our banking customers would enjoy an experience akin to shopping:

We invited potential customers to interact with the store and share their impressions:

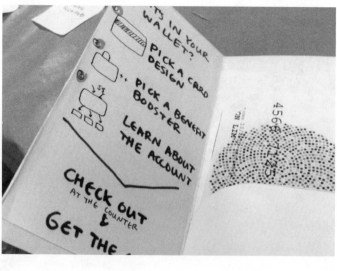

Direct observation changes everything.

As the initial concept was taking shape in the prototype store, we invited stakeholders to come and observe what customers were saying, doing and feeling while in the space. It was important for us that empathy was at the foundation of any research we did, in order to cultivate a customer-centric mindset and collective creativity among all the project's stakeholders.

Some ideas weren't welcomed by the internal stakeholders. For one, our idea of producing bank cards in multiple designs was criticised as it would increase operational costs without clear benefits. It was true that when customers were asked in a survey whether they were willing to pay more for a customisable card design, most ticked "No".

However, the very same stakeholder changed his view completely when we invited him to observe how young people behaved in the prototype store. He saw how much time they spent looking at the card designs – more than the features of the product! He saw how the designs actually became a conversation-starter for people coming in to browse.

When we look for ideas for innovation, surveys won't give us the Aha! moment. Observing people directly will. Because when we observe directly, it engages our senses and intuitions, not just logic. Empathy is a truly powerful ingredient for gaining a new perspective on how to innovate.

Make every research count

Here are 7 ways to turn every research practice into an opportunity to empathise with your customers. You will learn how to complement your current research with experiential methods, to ensure you get that all-important direct contact with your customers. Even if you talk to only a few customers about their experience, this direct interaction will have a profound impact on how you look at the business problem and how you approach the solution.

1. Direct interaction with your customers is key.

Direct interaction with customers allows us to engage our emotions and our senses, from sight and sound to even touch. In doing so, we get to observe, feel and empathise with every customer as a whole person and understand their deeper motivations.

Direct research methods such as observation, one-on-one interviews and ethnography aren't new; many organisations already use them as part of their research practice. **However, I sense that there is still a "fear" of direct interaction with customers.** Fear that customers may give a lot of feedback we can't handle. Fear that we may look unprofessional when we reveal our initial prototypes.

But the truth is, the result of direct interaction with customers is the total opposite of fear. I have lost count of the number of customers I have interviewed throughout my career, but I'm sure it's more than a thousand from all over the world. And each time, the interaction always revealed something that gave me and the team a fresh gush of energy and learning. At the end of research sessions, customers I had interviewed often told me: "You are actually spending so much time with customers? Your company seems to take customers really seriously."

When we talk to them, we get new perspectives and ideas.

When we show them our ideas, we get to find out what works and to kill those ideas that just don't resonate with them before we invest too much time and energy.

When we spend time with them, they can sense that our company takes their views seriously – and they appreciate it more than you think.

2. Have a one-on-one conversation.

Having a conversation with a customer is a great way to connect with them and to understand their needs and feelings. Some call this method "customer interviews", but I prefer the word "conversations", as it connotes the connection and genuineness of the interaction, as opposed to going through a standard interview questionnaire.

You might be familiar with the more common "focus group" method and wonder whether one-on-ones are necessary. It is important to note that the objective of a one-on-one conversation is very different from a focus group. In fact, some experts such as Karl Ronn, a former innovation executive at Procter & Gamble, have famously argued to ban focus groups, as they are not a suitable research method for uncovering people's contexts and needs.[2] Having a conversation with one person at a time allows us to go deeper and understand the nuances of emotions associated with a customer journey.

3. Collect stories.

"Insight" is different from what customers say. It is something we need to uncover based on the stories and data we gather.

Whenever you meet with a customer, maintain the frame of mind that you are there to **listen to their stories** as opposed to asking a set of pre-defined questions. **Stories are abundant sources of inspiration**. People love sharing their stories when they are in a comfortable environment and when they are heard. Listening to people's stories is a great way to empathise deeply with them.

In fact, we don't really know what we will get from the conversations. While it is important to establish some assumptions prior to research and prepare some questions to probe and inquire, having your customer share their story is the primary objective of this research method.

Companies like Amazon use a ton of metrics to measure success, but they also review "anecdotes" such as customer emails and feedback very seriously. Amazon's founder and CEO Jeff Bezos explains: "I've noticed when the anecdotes and the metrics disagree, the anecdotes are usually right. That's why it's so important to check that data with your intuition and instincts, and you need to teach that to executives and junior executives." The customer anecdotes collected through listening to their stories are more insightful than data.[3]

Stories are a reservoir of clues, hints and ideas that can point us to ways forward that we never even considered. Listening to customers' stories also allows us to go deeper into layers of unarticulated needs, which people are often not even conscious of themselves.

4. Talk to the extremes too.

There are several ways of recruiting customers (or employees) to talk to:

1. Selecting customers who present the most common profile of your customer base.

2. Selecting those who represent a range of personas (e.g. university student, new-to-workforce, experienced professional).

3. Selecting customers who are not typical, who have rather extremes traits (e.g. early adopters of new financial services apps, people who have never used mobile banking).

The combination of methods 1 and 2 is widely used. For example, when I was designing a mobile banking app, the team would look

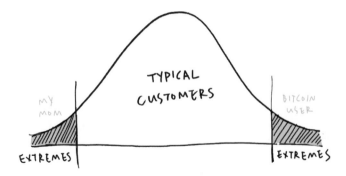

at our customer base, and identify the "typical mobile banking user" based on their usage frequency or their demographic.

You may wonder why method 3 – looking at the extremes – is useful. Say if we were working on an internet banking project, why would we talk to someone like my grandmother (laggard), who has never used a computer in her life? Or what's the point of talking to a user (early adopter) who doesn't use apps offered by the bank, but is actively using the latest financial apps?

Because the extremes can inspire us. From laggards we can discover the barriers to adopting new solutions and suss out opportunities to address their needs. My mom, who doesn't use a computer, is however an active user of KakaoTalk (South Korea's leading instant messaging service), and she can directly migrate into the payment service offered by KakaoPay without any barriers.

From early adopters, we can learn the gap between their needs and our product offerings, and predict the future behaviour of mass users. When Airbnb was first launched, their users were "unusually adventurous" people who didn't mind staying in a stranger's house. By designing for these early adopters, with constant iterations of the service design, we are now at the point where finding a place to stay through Airbnb is longer unusual behaviour at all. It has become mainstream, driving the shared economy.

5. Understand the customer as a whole person, not as a consumer.

We human beings love connecting with each other through conversation. Think about your first date. Or a situation when you met someone for the first time and tried to make a connection. In order to get to know someone, we typically start a conversation with small talk – asking about their family, job or hobbies.

In a conversation with a customer, approach it with this universal human behaviour in mind. Instead of diving straight into business, set aside time to get to know the person. This "warming-up" time not only creates a comfortable environment for customers to share their stories and feedback, you get to understand their context and deeper motivations for using your product or services.

6. Ask open-ended questions.

To inspire people to tell you their stories, ask open-ended questions instead of yes/no questions. Open-ended questions typically start with Who, What, When, Where, Why or How?

Use open-ended questions with your own team, too. For example, during an internal discussion or project meeting, ask a question to challenge the status quo and see how it can lead to an interesting discussion and spark new ways of looking at the problem: Why is this process complex? Why are we doing this particular thing in this particular way? When was the time we really loved using our own products?

Warren Berger, a journalist who has researched on the link between questioning and innovation, observed that brilliant change makers and innovators are all exceptionally good at asking the right questions. Open-ended questions train our mind to be curious and humble. It is a perspective shared by Richard Saul Wurman, founder of the TED conferences, who has said that good questioners tend to be aware of – and quite comfortable with – their own ignorance.

An ability to ask good questions needs to be trained; it may not come naturally to you. What is important is to give yourself permission to ask questions and to have a curious mind, before trying to find the "right" questions.

Growing up in South Korea, I don't recall myself ever asking the teachers open-ended questions, even when we were curious to know more. As young pupils, my friends and I were used to being asked closed-ended questions in our lessons and tests that asked us to choose one right answer, rather than describe why or how we came to that answer. As a result, even if we asked the teacher a question in class, it would only be to confirm if our understanding was correct. This mindset is still deeply ingrained in many of us as professionals, particularly in Asian cultures.

If you grew up in this kind of educational culture, asking open-ended questions can feel somewhat awkward. I struggled with this when I was starting my career. What I found to be very helpful was to have a set of questions or conversation prompts always on hand.

Here are some open-ended questions and prompts you can start with:

- Tell me about when you had (   ) experience?
- What was happening in your life around that time?
- Who was involved?
- What motivated you?
- How did you feel?
- How did you address that issue?
- Why did you feel that way?
- When was it?
- What did you do next?
- Why was it important to you?

Compile your own list of 10–20 open-ended questions. Make it yours by using the questions until they become natural to you. Practise asking your open-ended with friends and family. You may discover something enlightening about your spouse or close friends. Plus, having a habit of asking questions also makes us humble and keeps our mind curious.

How to conduct a simple, powerful interview

When conducting an interview, have an inverted triangle as your mental framework:

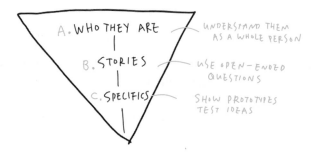

INTERVIEW STRUCTURE

A. WHO THEY ARE — UNDERSTAND THEM AS A WHOLE PERSON

B. STORIES — USE OPEN-ENDED QUESTIONS

C. SPECIFICS — SHOW PROTOTYPES TEST IDEAS

A. Start broad, so as to get to know the customer as a whole person. **B.** From there, collect stories which are likely to be related to high-level topics such as their overall journey, perception, motivation. **C.** Finally, you can go into the specifics. This could be a hypothesis or idea you want to test. You could also show prototypes at this stage to get the customer's feedback on what works and what doesn't.

This suggested sequence – starting broad and moving to specifics – is deliberate. Not only does it feel natural as a conversation, it is also designed for you to come away with both broad strategic findings as well as tactical-level findings. If an interview starts with specific questions (like a survey), it becomes very hard to uncover unarticulated needs and context, which are sources of innovative ideas.

7. Design ethnography: Go out, mingle and observe

By Dr Jung-Joo (JJ) Lee
Deputy Head of Research, Assistant Professor,
Division of Industrial Design, National University of Singapore

Dr Lee is an expert in empathic design methods and the author of *New Design Tools* (2018). She bridges traditional design education and service innovation. I love the work she has done in empowering students with deep design research methods to uncover innovation opportunities. I turned to her wisdom to introduce one of the most powerful research methods – design ethnography – which provides fundamental principles for customer engagement in the design process.

What is ethnography

Ethnography is an observational method originally developed in the social sciences to understand the behaviours, underlying norms and culture of people in a society. It was adopted in design in the late 1970s and gave rise to a new methodology called "design ethnography". Distinct from ethnography as practised in the social sciences, the core aim of design ethnography is to envision future opportunities, or "What if?". In addition to being a research method, it is also a design method.

I am often asked, "If you had to recommend just one method for people who want to understand their users, what would that be?". My answer is always, "You go out, mingle, and observe." This, in fact, is the fundamental mechanism of design ethnography.

Mingling and observing is the basic activity that we humans employ when we want to know more about other people. When we observe with a mindset of care and curiosity, we learn what people do in various situations, how they interact with their surroundings, what challenges they face, how they go about these challenges, etc.

How to observe

Many people seem to think that the key to design ethnography is to observe "objectively". They may draw an invisible line between the observer (myself) and the observed (the others). They may try to make their presence as inconspicuous as possible, like a fly on the wall, and intervene as little as possible in the situation.

Design ethnographers, however, believe that being an objective observer is a myth. Although one may try to be objective or influence-less, a human is not a machine. What we see (or what we choose to see), how we make sense of it, and how we convert it into data for our questions cannot be separated from our own interests, perspectives, and personal, cultural and social background. These factors shape the way we understand the world, and they shape the lens and interpretive logic of design ethnography, too.

To overcome the limitations of this non-objective position, design ethnographers look for the answer in empathy. If we cannot be objective after all, let us instead use the subjective aspects of human psychology as a tool to build empathy with the people we want to understand. Let me unfold how this is done in practice.

Awareness of your perspectives

One avenue is to make yourself aware of your subjective position. You could explicitly articulate your preconceptions, assumptions, interests and multiple backgrounds through activities like writing, drawing and conversing. In doing so, you recognise their possible influence on the way you observe and make sense of what you see. You then become sensitive to what you are observing, having internal reflections and conversations with yourself. Why does this look interesting to me? Is that what I already knew? Or am I glossing over interesting details with what I believe I know? What am I missing? Am I stereotyping them from my preconceptions?

While many talk about empathy so easily, genuine empathy can only be achieved once we know ourselves, our past experiences, beliefs, preconceptions and assumptions. Without this, the feeling you have towards others might be mere sympathy, not empathy. Sympathy is not necessarily wrong, but a strong feeling of sympathy can hinder you from unveiling complex dimensions of a problem. Empathy means having a humble mindset and never presuming that "I know exactly how you feel".

Self-ethnography

Professional ethnographers often practise self-ethnography, carefully observing themselves and writing about it. Self-ethnography helps externalise one's preconceptions and personal beliefs.

In the design process, self-ethnography can be carried out in a more visual way, e.g. by drawing a mind-map. This can be done individually or even as a team. In collective mind-mapping, team members can share their perspectives and interests, and check whether each other's observations and interpretations may be biased by their preconceptions. This shared awareness and understanding among team members facilitates more constructive data interpretation.

Once the mind-map has been created, display it where team members can regularly see it during the project, such as on the studio wall or near the coffee area. This provides a chance to continuously reflect on whether your work-in-progress findings are influenced by your preconceptions and expectations.

Participatory observation

Another principle of design ethnography is participatory observation, wherein the observer immerses himself in a situation, builds a relationship with the people in the situation, and learns their way of doing things. Through this process, the observer learns to see the situation from the members' point of view.

For example, to understand employees' experiences in a call centre, you could participate in the situation by serving as a call centre operator, learning the staff's methods and handling calls by yourself. In doing so, you would experience the situation as the employees do and build a genuine empathy for what drives their behaviours.

This kind of immersion is sometimes beyond what your project can afford in terms of resources or regulations. As an alternative, designers may use methods such as role-playing or an empathy workshop to achieve the same effect. Project stakeholders can act as users based on defined personas and scenarios and similarly have a bodily experience of the situation.

The seen and the unseen

The objective of observing or experiencing a scene from a member's point of view is to perceive the unseen beyond the seen. Here the "seen" refers to manifested behaviours, while the "unseen" are the underlying drivers, reasons or context – in other words, what makes people behave that way. When we observe, we are eventually interested in why people do something (the unseen), rather than just what they do (the seen). Discovery of why simplifies the complex dimensions and leads us to innovative solutions.

Jan Chipchase, a former principal scientist of Nokia Research Centre and the founder of design consultancy Studio D Radiodurans, shares a perfect example for this. In their work of design ethnography, they often looked into what people carry with them everyday. They identified three objects that are commonly found in people's bags and pockets: a key, money, and a mobile phone. They dug into the meanings of these objects, to understand what they mean to people. A key, money, and a phone – they all represent survival. This is the unseen why. Having perceived this, your design direction then becomes set around how to provide the experience of security, not around a key, a wallet or a phone.

Discovery of why also ensures the reliability of your data. Understanding the contexts and drivers of people's behaviours can be more powerful than conducting an online survey of 500 people that would only tell you the average, not a true picture of individuals. This is why you can trust results from observing as few as ten people.

Ultimately, design ethnography is a great training tool for developing an empathic mindset and sensitivity. With these in place, whichever specific method you choose to use, you will have the eyes to see the situation from the users' point of view and the power to access the unseen dimension behind users' behaviour.

Don't do research alone. Involve your stakeholders.

Very often, research is carried out by a team of specialists, after which the findings and insights are shared with the broader group of people in the organisation. While this is a common practice, it is time for a fundamental shift.

The method I introduce here is Experience Labs, a laboratory environment for your stakeholders to directly observe, hear and feel what your customers experience. As we saw in the previous chapter, direct contact with customers is incredibly powerful for creating empathy among your stakeholders and helping them to look at business problems from a fresh perspective. The approach of Experience Labs contrasts with the typical engagement of stakeholders, where research findings are shared through a deck of slides.

How Experience Labs work

Experience Labs consists of two parts: (1) A one-on-one conversation with a customer, which often includes the testing of ideas; and (2) Stakeholders observing the interviews from another room and then discussing the findings together.

1. Have a conversation with a customer to uncover their needs

Set aside one hour for a one-on-one conversation with a customer (as introduced in Chapter 3.1). Start the conversation by asking about them and gathering their stories around the research topic. The objective is to understand their context, environment, motivations and behaviours. Towards the later part of interview, the interviewer can test more specific ideas or hypotheses. At this stage, showing prototypes can further facilitate the process.

2. Bring your stakeholders closer to your customers

Here is the important part. Prepare another room for your colleagues and stakeholders – people in your organisation who have an interest in the project and who are the decision-makers. While the interview is taking place, have them observe the interview (e.g. via a video link) and write down what they observe about the customer, their needs, and their feedback to the prototypes.

Experience Labs: Project stakeholders observing an interview

After each interview, conduct a 30-minute wrap-up session with the stakeholders, to make sense of what they observed and learned. Because these stakeholders represent different departments, from marketing to operations to legal, you will find that you are able to capture a much more holistic picture than if you were doing the research alone. Each stakeholder will have been paying attention to different aspects of the interview, focusing on those that have an implication on their area of work.

More importantly, in directly observing the interviews, your stakeholders will begin to see the problem differently and will want to change the status quo. During the wrap-up session, important decisions are shaping up, from big strategic directions to immediately actionable ideas. By providing your stakeholders an environment to observe customers with empathy, you help them see the need for change. **What happens in this room is incredibly powerful.**

FAQ about Experience Labs

Q1. How many people do we need to interview?

Experience Labs aim to uncover the depth, rather than breadth, of consumer needs and behaviour. This means you don't need to talk to too many people. As Nielsen Norman Group's research revealed, talking to as few as five people will reveal the most critical findings.[4] Of course, the more people you talk to, the more findings you'll have, but the curve gets significantly flatter after that.

I recommend interviewing 5–8 people per round. After the first round, gather the findings, learn from them and improve on the concept. Then run another round of 5–8 people. Repeat this until you get clarity and confidence on your project direction.

Q2. At which stage should Experience Labs be conducted?

Experience Labs should definitely be run in the early stages of a project. This allows you to start with customers' point of view in mind. The initial stage is also crucial in shaping the project's scope and vision. Therefore, multiple rounds of Experience Labs need to be planned for this stage.

As the project proceeds, there will be times when injecting a fresh dose of empathy is necessary. Rob Ballantine, a digital leader for the healthcare industry, shares his experience running Experience Labs in the middle of agile sprints: "When the whole development team sat to observe the users – doctors and nurses – giving feedback to our system, it completely changed the energy of the team. Based on the observation, we reviewed the product backlog, and removed and revised the items. That was very effective and engaging!"

Q3. What facilities are required to set up Experience Labs?

At OCBC Bank, we built the Experience Labs by dedicating one room for the interviews, and one room for the observers.

The interview room was designed to feel like someone's living room to create a comfortable atmosphere. The sofa area was used in the first phase of the interview to gather stories. We would then move to the desk area to show them the prototypes.

The observer room was designed with two large video screens and a good audio system. The walls were made of materials that allowed materials such as prototypes or flipcharts to be pinned up.

However, it is not a must to have a custom-built technical facility like this. When I was with Credit Suisse, we used two adjacent meeting rooms and set up a video camera in the interview room and connected the cable to the monitor in the observers' room. The outcome was equally effective.

When running research outside the office, it's often not possible to set up separate rooms for the interviews and observers. In such situations, the observers can be placed in the interview room itself. Care must be taken to plan the seating arrangements of the interviewer, the customer and the observers, to ensure the customer feels comfortable and the interviews are carried out well.

Q4. How many rounds should I plan?

This very much depends on the scope or the stage of the project, but the rule of thumb from my experience is to go to at least the third round of iteration, which often brings a breakthrough idea to the table.

Q5. Do interviewees know they are being observed?

It is important to let your interviewees know all the logistical details, e.g. how long it will take, what will happen during the interview. This includes letting them know that there are observers listening and taking notes. I like to position the observers as my colleagues who are very interested to hear customers' stories and collect customer feedback.

Q6. Should I record the interview sessions so that I can show them to my stakeholders?

Sometimes it's not logistically possible to have everyone in the room (e.g. due to conflicting schedules). Recordings are a good way of capturing the proceedings for documentation and sharing, but do not rely solely on them. Even if it's a small group of observers, aim to make use of direct observation and immediate debriefing. The first-hand impressions from non-verbal cues (such as gestures and expressions) observed directly are very powerful. Experience Labs are best experienced "live".

Be inspired by your customers, but distinguish between data and insight

Lessons learned from Shoes of Prey

Finding a perfect pair of high heels we can feel comfortable and confident in is many a career woman's dream. That's when I found Shoes of Prey, an online store selling customisable shoes. I could choose the type of shoe I wanted (pumps, sandals, even sneakers) and then choose the colour, materials, finishing-touch items such as buckles, etc. What I loved the most was that I could decide the height of the heels, as well as whether I wanted a slightly wider cut or narrower cut.

Their online customisation tool was joy to use, with a dynamic visualisation of my custom configuration. I had fun designing many pairs of shoes, and saved them in the shopping cart. Out of over 20 pairs I designed, I ended up ordering five. When they arrived, I admired the lovely boxes and wrapping, and the hand-written thank-you note. The attention to detail made my experience great. Except for one pair that didn't fit so well, the rest of them became my go-to high heels.

I wasn't the only one who was so enthusiastic about this new way of buying shoes. The Sydney-based start-up broke even two months after launching, according to Business of Fashion, and by 2014 it was hitting multimillion-dollar revenue goals and had designed over 4 million pairs of shoes. In 2017, sales reportedly hit $115 million.

But about a year ago, I heard the sad news that Shoes of Prey had closed its operations in summer 2018 and reported a loss of $24 million. The founders were interviewed and they candidly shared what went wrong.

Get fuelled by empathy   63

One of their biggest mistakes was not recognising the gap between what customers said they wanted and what they truly wanted. In the market research they did, consumers told them they welcomed customisation, and this led the founders to the belief that customisation was the future of fashion.

But what the consumers really wanted – perhaps even without being conscious of it – was being inspired by trends and influencers, and adopting their style. So, in fact, as co-founder Jodie Fox put it, "What they were consciously telling us and what they subconsciously wanted were effectively polar opposites."[5]

That's how important it is to get your research right. For co-founder Michael Fox, the key takeaway was this: "There are customer research methods that enable you to peel back the layers of psychology to understand what a customer truly wants. While this type of customer research is difficult to get right and the results aren't always clear cut, if I'm ever attempting to change consumer behaviour again, I will do this."[6]

As a fan of Shoes of Prey, I'm sad to see they're no longer in business. But at the same time I'm impressed by the founders' courageous acceptance of their failures and candid sharing of their start-up journey.

From this story, we can draw some extremely valuable lessons on research methods. Above all, we need to choose the right methods to suit the particular research objective. Customers are the source of inspiration, but what customers say they want may not be the answer.

First, "data" and "insights" are different.

A key aspect of improving the effectiveness of your research practice is to distinguish between data and insight. How are they different? Let's say you've just received a report from your UX research team and it includes this statement:

> "People tend to press this button when it's designed with an icon."

Is this data, or an insight? (Pick your answer before reading on.)

Data is a fact. It's something we gather from our research or data analytics tools. Data tells you what is happening. **Insight, on the other hand, is an enlightening new discovery about customers' needs and behaviour or the market**. An insight tells us why things are happening.

Now, going back to the question, is "People tend to press this button when it's designed with an icon" data or insight?

It is data. It is an observation of what happened. It does not reveal anything about why the user may behave that way.

When I posed this question in a lecture, some people said the statement should be considered an insight, because it expressed a finding and they'd seen similar statements presented as insights in their organisation. They felt it wasn't "data", because data is about statistics and figures.

This is a common misconception. **Data doesn't just refer to numbers. In fact, data can be findings and behaviours we have observed or facts we have gathered from research**; it can even be what customers say they want, e.g. "We want customisable shoes."

Not challenging mere observations with an inquiring mind and taking data as insight is one of the biggest reasons for the gap between the amount of research done and the lack of new ideas.

Second, there is gap between what people say and their actual behaviour.

This is a research trap that many companies fall into. It happens when there is insufficient clarity in the research objective.

Traditionally, so-called "quantitative market research" (e.g. surveys) was used to **validate ideas** before launching a product or marketing initiative. This method gives fairly clear answers regarding users' needs, and works very well in known markets or with a known product type. However, it is a weak method when you're looking to create a new product type for a new market.

To uncover ideas for innovation, we need to do research in a way that allows us to **get inspired** by our customers, rather than merely look for validation.

Imagine a scenario where, during your research for a new product, customers tell you that they want it to have a particular function, "Function X". At this point, the approach you need to take is to uncover the why behind this data point by asking follow-up questions:

- What aspects of Function X make customers want it?

- In what kind of circumstances do customers want Function X?

- What emotional or social needs does the customer have in wanting Function X?

- What are the jobs that customers are trying to get done by using Function X? (These questions will be discussed in detail in Chapter 5.)

People may verbally articulate their reasons, but their deeper motivations or emotional needs may remain unspoken. **It is the researcher's job to observe the context, collect stories and synthesise data points to draw further inferences.** Don't take customers' verbal answers at face value; always try and look deeper into their behaviour, aspirations and emotions. This is where the real insights lie.

Steve Jobs famously said that he didn't believe in market research, because consumers aren't able to describe what they want. I'm sure Apple was doing a lot of market research nevertheless, but Jobs' quote serves to highlight the limitations of traditional research methods. It is a company's job to imagine and design products or services that its customers will want, even if they don't know it yet. And that's something that Apple has done so very well.

Synthesise to uncover insights

Synthesis is the sense-making process of turning data into knowledge, and knowledge into insights. It's what makes design thinking feel magical, because this is where new insights are born.

Unlike other design activities such a journey mapping or prototyping, the process and outcome of synthesis are not as visible. There is also the assumption that only very gifted experts can synthesise complex data points into insights. It is true that synthesis is hard. **But it is a vital part of the innovation process.** We need to put a lot of effort into this stage of the design process, in order to avoid drawing misleading conclusions from our data points, as Shoes of Prey unfortunately did.

Intuition is allowed, because we empathised.

Synthesis is different from analysis. While logical thinking is certainly involved in synthesis, what distinguishes it from analysis is the use of intuition. Many people in my classes struggle with the idea that intuition can be allowed in such an important process as identifying innovation opportunities for their organisations. "Isn't this then a subjective conclusion?" they ask me.

Our intuition is rooted in the wealth of inner resources that we have accumulated through our knowledge and the experiences in our personal and professional lives.

Synthesis is a human technique. We acknowledge that we have our personal judgements and that we have to work with limited information. Yet we connect the dots of different data points to generate new knowledge. In this process, we need to tap on our intuition – how we feel about the problem and our observations from customers' stories, what connections we see even if there is no clear logical evidence.

Think of the moment you made the decision to marry someone. How did you make such a big decision? What process did you go through? Did you have a spreadsheet to analyse all the traits and variables? More importantly, what "sample size" did you deal with? Were you able to obtain and test out a statistically significant sample size, date and analyse each candidate, and compare the results?

Probably not. You listened to your intuition to make this important decision. At the risk of stretching the comparison, the process of synthesis is somewhat like this. It is a sophisticated human technique that draws on our knowledge, experiences and even our gut-feel with all the data points we have gathered, to show us the way forward.

How to synthesise

1. Synthesis must be done with people from different backgrounds

Approach synthesis as a team sport. Make use of the collective wisdom and domain knowledge of people from different job roles, educational backgrounds, etc. This will vastly enrich the outcome of synthesis. Don't rely on a few individuals or external consultants to synthesise alone; doing it that way, you miss out on harnessing organisational brain power and creativity.

2. Prior to synthesis, people must have had the opportunity to empathise with customers

Earlier in the chapter, we discussed how empathy is directly connected to our ability to reframe. The reason why intuition is allowed in synthesis lies here. People who will be bringing their intuition to the table must have been given an opportunity to empathise with customers prior to the synthesis session. This can be done through meeting customers or observation at Experience Labs (introduced in Chapter 3.2).

3. Find "good enough" connections, rather than the "right" connections

Visualise a detective's wall in a thriller movie. The wall is pasted with a collage of newspaper articles, photos of suspects, maps, receipts, etc. The detectives try to come up with the best predictions by connecting the dots of what happened in the case. They may work as a team, looking at the wall together and discussing possible scenarios. When they form some sort of enlightening conclusion, they immediately drive off to a site to confirm if their provisional conclusion is right, and to gather more evidence.

When synthesising data points to uncover insights, look for the best predictions through establishing "good enough" connections between the data points, rather than trying to find the one "right" answer. Allow people to think in terms of "maybe", and produce many predictions. Attempting to find the killer insight on your first guess is extremely hard; it takes an iterative process.

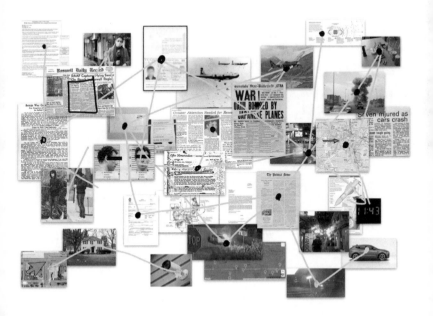

4. Externalise the process of synthesis

While sense-making is an internal process (at this very moment as you are reading this book, you are having a sense-making moment), synthesis is an external process where we involve other people. To maximise the effect of synthesis and to unleash collective brain power, externalise the process as much as possible.[5]

Externalising means, first of all, taking your thoughts out of your brain and writing them down. Next, if you keep your notes on your computer or your phone, take them out of these digital devices and write them on some physical media such as post-its. Ideally, find a large wall space for the team to put up their post-its – this really allows everyone to pick up patterns, connect the dots, and form insights.

At the time of writing, in the midst of the Covid-19 pandemic crisis, virtual collaboration is becoming the new norm. If you are working virtually, try using collaboration tools such as Zoom's whiteboard, Miro or Mural, which emulate the physical collaboration environment and hence encourage team members to externalise their thoughts.

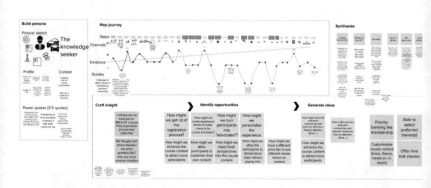

Collaborating and synthesising virtually using Mural

5. Use both unstructured and structured methods

I personally like to lead a synthesis session with unstructured matters first. After externalising all the data points on a board, I ask people what they find interesting. Whenever an interesting data point is identified, this means something even if we don't know the reason why yet. Our intuition is responding to that piece of data we gathered.

After letting the mind freely connect the dots, we can then introduce certain methods to structure the next step of the process. Some structured methods are:

- **Clustering and finding themes:** Identify any common themes that emerge. Add a post-it with the name of the theme, and move all data points that are related to the theme into a cluster around it.

- **Insight-o-meter:** Label your findings in terms of how much each one enlightens you, from *Duh* (That's obvious), to *OK* (I get it) to *Aha* (I never thought about this before!).

- **Looking for contradictions:** Cluster the data points into what customers say, do, think and feel. From there, identify contradicting behaviours or feelings. When contradictions are identified, we are likely to have identified opportunities to solve the tension.

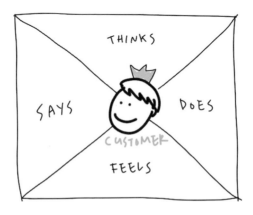

An empathy map can help us identify contradictions

6. Give it time and a conducive environment

The process of gathering data, synthesising and crafting insights takes time. It requires deep thinking and many rounds of discussion. Don't overlook the power of the environment to boost the team's ability to synthesise. For example, secure a morning session, if possible, to tap on team members' fresh morning energy. A room with good daylight will make people feel good and think sharp.

Relentlessly pursue reframing

At the end of the synthesis process, the aim is to discover new perspectives of looking at the problem, customer or solution you had. New perspectives allow us to spot new opportunities and better ways of dealing with existing problems. In other words, synthesis is followed by reframing.

Let's first look at some examples of reframing and see what difference this method can make in shaping a business strategy or project direction.

Coffee business → People business serving coffee

"At Starbucks, I've always said we're not in the coffee business serving people, but we're in the people business serving coffee," said Howard Schulz, Chairman, President and CEO of Starbucks. This quote captures perfectly how powerful a company's mission can become by shifting its perspective. Instead of running a "coffee business", designing experiences as a "people business service coffee" made the Starbucks experience we know today.

Feed them content → Help them generate their own knowledge

In 2018, an internal study at OCBC Bank revealed the need for upskilling the bank's advisors to better serve a certain group of customers. The initial reaction of senior stakeholders was to build a content app for the advisors based on the knowledge gap identified. Before building the app, we spoke to the bank advisors to better understand their current experience, and to learn how they acquired knowledge needed for their work.

After spending time with bank advisors across three branches, we discovered some very interesting behaviours. The advisors communicated a lot among themselves, exchanging ideas and challenges over water-cooler conversations and WhatsApp group chats. To them, the notion of knowledge was based on real-life situations, not only being book smart; they were genuinely interested in how other advisors solved certain problems in servicing customers. The idea of "tribe leaders" naturally emerged, with team leaders generously sharing their experiences, as well as certain advisors emerging as experts on particular financial products.

This observation inspired the team to reframe the problem. From "Feed them content to fill the knowledge gap", the problem statement was reframed as "Help them generate their own knowledge".

With that, the project direction completely changed from the initial plan of building a content app to designing a forum. The new forum app, Ask Anyone, has become the place where the advisors initiate a lot of conversations, learn from one another, and harness the collective wisdom of the entire branch network.

How to reframe

1. First, frame your assumptions

Before the research begins, articulate all the assumptions your company or team has regarding the problem statement. Assumptions are mainly found in three areas: (1) **customer** hypothesis – what we think we know about customers; (2) **problem** hypothesis – what we think is the problem; and (3) **solution** hypothesis – what solution may solve the problem.[8]

I have observed two interesting phenomena over the years. First, many projects start with some ideas for solutions already in mind. A solution might have been offered by a senior manager before the research even started, or formed by the competitive landscape.

Second, the initial problem statement is often not challenged. While a problem exists when initiating a project, that doesn't mean the problem is the right one to solve. It could be framed a certain way due to the time pressure of wanting to execute things as soon as possible, or there has not been the right process or mental space to step back and challenge it.

To avoid this pitfall, I recommend framing "requirements" as "assumptions". While others are locked in by requirements, you are able to interrogate these assumptions and reject them if necessary. This will give you a distinct competitive advantage in dealing with innovation projects and save precious organisational resources in focusing on solving the right problem.

2. Empathise with your users

As discussed in the previous section, there is a strong connection between empathy and reframing. When we walk in the customer's shoes by having direct contact with them, observing them and listening to their stories, we naturally acquire new framings. This is a compelling business case for research practices in organisations to embrace more of the direct research methods we discuss in this book.

3. Synthesis is where the magic happens

Look for patterns and themes using the techniques of synthesis discussed earlier. The quality of synthesis with the right group of people will be the key in identifying areas for reframing.

4. Create contrasts from the initial assumptions

During the synthesis process, go back to the initial problem statement and all the assumptions you articulated in Step 1. Use the initial assumptions to look for contrasts between your assumptions and what you discovered about customers' needs and behaviours. Searching for this shift in perspective can yield interesting and valuable insights. Also note, these insights can be continuously iterated and reframed as the design process progresses.

5. Have a positive mindset and keep searching

While using the discussed techniques, wear the hat of an optimist. Have faith that there are always areas for reframing, and keep searching for them even if you can't seem to see them at first glance. Those who seek shall find new perspectives.

Chapter 4
Dance with complexity

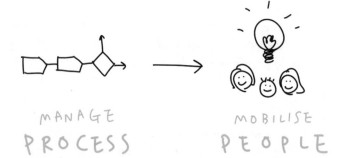

MANAGE
PROCESS

MOBILISE
PEOPLE

Simplicity and complexity need each other.
The more complexity there is in the market,
the more that something simpler stands out.
— John Maeda[1]

PICTURE A BALLROOM DANCING SCENE.

Imagine two dance partners performing an elegant English waltz, or perhaps an upbeat foxtrot. When we watch a great dance performance, we know that behind the scenes there has been a great deal of hard work: understanding the origins of genres, mastering techniques, working through the dynamics between partners, and loads of practice.

When I was a keen ballroom dance student, I worked very hard to master my steps, because I wanted to dance like Jennifer Lopez and Richard Gere in the movie, "Shall We Dance?". But of course I was far from being like her, and I often blamed my dance partner for not being skilful enough! It was quite frustrating for both of us.

One day, during practice, my teacher stopped me and told me something that changed my approach completely. It was to respect my partner's role and his space. And to always be in tune with my partner's subtle cues before deciding on my next move. It wasn't simply mastering my own technique that would make a great outcome; it was about learning to work together and trusting my partner's creativity.

Why am I talking about dancing when we need to talk about complexity?

Firstly, it is to emphasise the "people dynamics" in managing complexity. One of the key lessons I learned from my simplicity journey is that no matter how complex a topic is, it can be simplified by bringing people together. These people can be your project team members, subject matter experts, internal stakeholders, external ecosystem partners, and even industry regulators. It is crucial to work with the right people to understand the complex subject and to work out the creative solutions together, the same way I had to work with my dance partner to break down complex steps and understand the techniques. Because simplicity is achieved only through a thorough examination of the subject matter. People's knowledge and willingness hold the key to successful simplification.

Secondly, it is to highlight the discipline behind creativity. Great dance performances are not the outcome of random creativity. Contrary to common belief, creativity doesn't belong to a few people in free-flowing form. Instead, particularly in the business context, creativity is about discipline – having an intent, structures, methods, and striving to be proficient at it through lots of practice. In fact, creativity can be "farmed" when we have the discipline and methods to mobilise the people we work with.

Let's shift our approach from the technical aspect of change (process) to the soft aspect, which is people. In this chapter, we will discuss methods to unleash the creativity of your "dance partners" to solve complex problems together.

In this chapter

4.1 The more complex the product, the more the opportunities.
4.2 From process-oriented to people-centred.
4.3 Cultivate creativity with discipline.
4.4 Co-create with experts.
4.5 Visualise complexity.
4.6 Concretise the abstract through prototyping.
4.7 Be a pain sponge.

The more complex the product, the more the opportunities.

The layers of complexity

When we feel something is complex – whether it's a topic or a product – chances are the complexity comes from one or more of the "layers" surrounding it. I call these the Layers of Complexity:

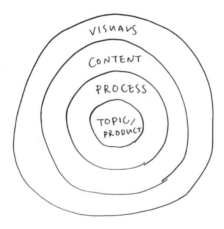

1. **The visual layer:** This is when a topic or product looks or feels complex. It's the way information is presented and visual design is used.

2. **The content layer:** The way things are communicated is hard to understand, or the features presented are hard to use (e.g. content and functions on a website).

3. **The process layer:** Getting things done requires many steps or a lot of effort (e.g. the process of buying a house).

4. **The product/topic layer:** The topic or product itself is complex (e.g. insurance products, legal matters or scientific topics).

These layers are naturally interlinked. When the topic itself is complex, the following layers such as process, content and visuals tend to be complex as well. A complex-looking form typically mirrors the complex internal processes.

This also means simplifying only the outer visual layer without examining the deeper layers of complexity is rarely possible. And the biggest impact will be created if we are able to simplify all the layers of complexity.

Today's consumers do not tolerate complexity.

In the past, when the topic itself was complex, people generally accepted the complex process, content and visuals that came with it. For example, when we take up a new insurance policy, we accept that a lot of paperwork is required, because insurance businesses are supposed to be complex. And because people accept the complexity of the product, process, content and visuals, they may buy an insurance product without fully understanding it! Complexity can be dangerous.

However, the acceptance level of complexity is about to change. Or rather, it is already changing rapidly. People today are increasingly less likely to accept complexity. In the insurance industry, for example, new players entering the market have shown customers that buying insurance doesn't have to be complicated at all. The simple customer experience they offer has made consumers expect the same of other insurance companies.

Simplifying the layers of complexity

GoBear, a comparison site for financial products, was founded in Singapore in 2014 and has since grown into Asia's leading financial services platform. It is a great example of a new entrant offering simple experiences and revolutionising the way things are done in an industry.

Compare banking and insurance in seconds

Easily search and compare hundreds of products from dozens of providers to find what you really need.

The topic layer

The founders of GoBear had a deep understanding of how confused consumers felt in dealing with buying insurance products, particularly in comparing products and in choosing the right insurance for them. Inspired by these pain points, they were determined to help consumers improve their financial health by simplifying the process of comparing and buying an insurance product.

The process layer

Not only did they make the process of comparing different financial products simpler, they worked with their partners to make the entire customer journey – from searching to comparing to buying – seamless.

The content layer

Their value proposition was to offer unbiased views on different products and helpful financial literacy content. The content is written as if the company's mascot, Bear, is speaking directly to you. Bear is unbiased, speaks in simple language, and can sometimes be funny too. Even the form is designed to humanise the experience by taking a conversational tone as opposed to operational form-filling.

The visual layer

The website's graphic interface is simple and welcoming. Unlike many financial services websites, it has ample white space that gives room to breathe. The friendly look and feel is expressed through the choice of typeface and the consistent presence of the bear. The brand colour, green, is sparingly used to highlight the most important content, in order to create focus.

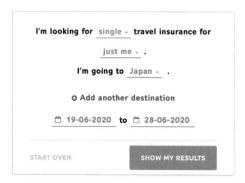

GoBear started with one product category: travel insurance in Singapore. They have now successfully expanded into seven countries, offering a broad range of financial products in categories such as credit cards, home loans, money transfers and investment platforms, and have chalked up more than 55 million site visitors.[2] GoBear's story shows that we need to embrace the somewhat counterintuitive fact that the more complex a business or industry is, the more opportunities you have to differentiate your business by making it simpler.

From process-oriented to people-centred

Any innovation initiative requires change. But as we all know, change is hard. Human beings are resistant to change, because change represents the unknown, and the unknown is scary.

If you are leading innovation, digital transformation or customer experience initiatives, what you are essentially doing is making change. Your job title may not include the word "change", but your success lies in your ability to drive the desired change. This is known as change management.

Change management = Changing individuals

Professor Vibha Gaba at INSEAD suggests that to change organisations, we have to change individuals, sometimes including ourselves. Typically, change management comes down from the top, or from a dedicated change agent, in the form of "process change". It can be adopting a new work process or an organisation structure change. Instead of dealing with these process changes, we need to shift our focus to people. Because change happens when people change. After all, change management is about influencing people, and to influence people, we first have to understand them, respect them and connect with them.

When I started my job as a customer experience designer in OCBC Bank 10 years ago, spending time with key stakeholders over coffee, lunch or drinks really helped me better understand their goals, concerns and context. The time with them provided me with a solid foundation to work with them and drive change initiatives together for many years to come. When we, as change agents, better understand stakeholders' perspective and needs, we can be smarter about how to introduce and execute the change.

Another thing I learned is that the reason why change management is hard is not necessarily because people do not agree with the outcome of the change. Often, we encounter resistance to change from individuals because the change was imposed upon them, rather than involving them. So it is critical to engage with key individuals such as the process owners and subject matter experts on solving specific problems together. Instead of having "meetings" – where we sit down and talk – approach each meeting as a "work session" that is designed with a clear intent and structure to harness people's knowledge and creativity. Let's look at the methods for proactively designing such work sessions.

Cultivate creativity with discipline

Human-centred design – also referred to as design thinking – is an approach to solving problems and creating solutions with human needs at the centre, using a designer's way of thinking. The core mechanism of design thinking is the combination of divergent and convergent thinking:

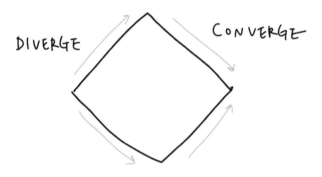

A divergent process refers to seeking and generating ideas with an open mind. Activities such as meeting customers for a conversation, brainstorming ideas and testing are great examples of divergent processes. It feels intuitive and liberating.

A convergent process is then bringing rigorous, logical thinking to all the data points you have gathered and options you have generated. Activities such as sense-making, prioritisation and decision-making are examples of convergent processes. It feels rigorous and analytical.

I have found, through the numerous workshops I've conducted in my career, that structuring group discussions into divergent and convergent thinking provides the conditions for people to flourish. They start generating much more creative ideas and making smarter decisions. Creativity lies in both divergent and convergent processes. Knowing when to diverge or converge, and effectively facilitating activities, will define the quality of the process as well as the outcome.

Don't think out of the box. Give people different boxes to think with.

People often think of creativity as the ability to think "out of the box". During brainstorming sessions, people are encouraged to think "out of the box" to generate creative ideas. In reality, however, only very few people can do that. When we work in a group, the better strategy is to give people different boxes to think with.

This means, instead of giving one topic for a brainstorming session, we create multiple topics for people to generate ideas on. For example, if the initial brainstorming topic was "How to redefine the role of banking branches", instead of asking people to think out of the box, create a variety of "boxes" for people to generate ideas within. The boxes can be created to reflect different aspects or opportunities, such as:

- How might we make the branch a fun place? (customer experience)

- How might we better serve customers with children, or retirees, or business owners? (segment strategy)

- How might we integrate digital and physical services? (channel strategy)

Once the different boxes are created, focus on each one for about 15 minutes, brainstorming ideas as a group, before moving on to the next box. This way of generating ideas will yield far more ideas than spending the whole hour trying to think out of the one box.

Create "just right"-sized boxes.

When creating these boxes to generate ideas, ensure the size of the box is "just right". When the topic identified in the box is too broad, it is as difficult as asking people to think out of the box. When the topic is too specific, there is no room for generating ideas.

IDEO, one of the world's leading design and consulting firms, promoted "The Goldilocks Principle", borrowed from the fairy tale of a little girl Goldilocks visiting a house of three bears.

JUST RIGHT
FOR IDEATION

How might we improve air travel?

TOO BIG. ABSTRACT

How might we get passengers to use their own device?

TOO SPECIFIC

How might we make air travel delightful for parents with children?

JUST RIGHT.

In this example, the question "How might we improve air travel?" is so generic and broad that it's very hard to generate ideas. On the other hand, "How might we get passengers to use their own tech instead of bothering flight attendants?" is too specific, even uninspiring. The "just right" question would be "How might we make air travel more delightful and convenient for parents and children?". The moment you encounter this statement, don't you immediately have some images or ideas springing into mind? This is the "just right" size of box.

Co-create with experts

Work with experts early in the process.

Achieving simplicity is different from developing a simplistic solution. Simplicity is the thoughtful result of a thorough examination of the subject matter and a rigorous creative process. In both divergent and convergent processes, we need experts who possess domain knowledge or subject matter expertise, both inside the organisation and outside. Typically they come from domains such as technology, product or operations.

In highly regulated environments, such as financial services or healthcare, working with legal and compliance experts will be key in the creative process. I've seen many simplicity initiatives fail due to regulatory or operational constraints. I often hear from business heads that their teams couldn't obtain the approval from legal or compliance. So instead of only approaching these "approval" parties in the later stages of a project, involve them earlier in the process.

The goal is to "co-create" rather than "get approval".

Think of these regulatory and approval bodies as experts who are helping you co-create. Use them to clarify your thoughts and refine your offering, so that you can create sound options that will meet business needs, customer needs as well as regulatory requirements. Personally, I have observed that legal and compliance experts are very creative and helpful in generating ideas when they are involved early in the process. Some are also keen to change the status quo themselves!

Natalie Koh, who has been leading Plain English initiatives in OCBC Bank for many years, shares that establishing a co-creating relationship with the legal team is key: "It is important to get them on the same page as us, and not perceive that they are against us when they disagree. We assure them that while we aim for simplicity and clarity, it is also our intent to safeguard customers' and the bank's interest through clear communication."

People become part of the story when they co-create.

In the middle of the 2008 global financial crisis, as a customer experience specialist at Credit Suisse, I was tasked with simplifying the fact sheet of structured derivatives – one of the most complicated investment product categories at that time. The objective was to make it easy for customers to understand this class of products, and to ensure the content was accurate (not over-simplified) and legally sound.

In order to achieve this, I needed a group of experts representing lawyers, compliance officers, product specialists and investment officers. They had the subject matter knowledge I needed to work towards a solution.

But there were so many challenges standing in the way of working with them. Each party had different perspectives on how to solve the problem, and they were all extremely busy people. Scheduling a long workshop with all of them would be very difficult. We would need to have an intensive work session that delivered a tangible solution at the end of it, rather than just a discussion session to hear everyone's opinions. I couldn't afford to waste anybody's time.

What I designed was a work session that I now call "co-creation". The main idea was to enable everyone in the group to be an active problem-solver rather than a mere contributor. **By moving away from discussing problems to channelling our energy towards co-creating solutions,** within 2 hours we were able to arrive at a common vision *and* produce several prototypes to test with customers. All the stakeholders were pleased with the outcome and with the very productive and creative session.

How were we able to achieve all that so fast?

- The session was positioned as "co-creation", rather than as an "expert review meeting". I discovered that people have genuine motivation to solve the problem and do the right thing when the setup is right. And as they poured their knowledge, energy and creativity into the solutions, they started to take ownership of the solution ideas. And because of that, they become ambassadors of change.

- Solving problem *visually* makes a difference when we work together as a group. This can be in the form of a rough sketch or a mock-up, which allows the group to discuss concretely and develop ideas together, as opposed to just verbalising. This method is called "prototyping" (which I will explain in Chapter 4.6).

People embrace what they create. When people are co-creators, they become part of its story.[3] Co-create with experts to develop powerful solutions that meet the needs of your business and your customers, as well as regulatory needs.

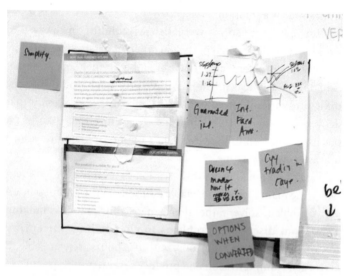

An example of prototyping during a co-creation session – a combination of a rough sketch, cut-outs from a document and post-it notes. This level of "low-resolution" prototyping is very effective for sharing ideas during a co-creation session.

How to design a co-creation session

Create empathy and a sense of urgency: Give your gathered experts an opportunity to empathise with how customers feel about the problem, for example by starting the session with customer feedback in various formats, e.g. statistics, or even better, customer interview scenes that show the problems your group needs to solve.

Individual reflections: It's important to give individuals time to reflect on the problems, and for experts to express their thoughts at the beginning of the session. In order to save time, I suggest doing this in writing through a predefined questionnaire, followed by a brief sharing. As everyone will have had a chance to express their views in writing, you don't need to ask and listen to everyone's answer; you may highlight a few thoughts, and then move on to the active stage of co-creation.

Plan working groups: Divide the group into teams of 3–5 people, ideally with each team having a good mix of roles and backgrounds.

Structure topics of discussion: To have the most productive discussion, the session needs to be deliberately designed, rather than allowing people to freely discuss on the given topic. When the topic is complex and sensitive to deal with, a framework such as "The Six Thinking Hats" can be very useful. The idea is to improve the thinking process by deliberately challenging the group to think about the various aspects of an issue in turn: neutral facts (white hat), how they feel about the issue (red hat), pessimistic judgements (black hat), positive outlooks (yellow hat), required processes (blue hat), and creative ideas (green hat). When different groups come together to discuss a serious business problem, blaming or fear of sharing ideas can occur. By actively facilitating what to talk about in a certain sequence, you can ease anxiety and lead the group to reach a creative solution in a structured manner.

Produce ideas in concrete form: While the dialogue is taking place, task the teams to produce their ideas in concrete form (prototyping). The idea is to activate their hands to enhance thinking, and to use visuals to create a shared vision.

Conclude with a positive outlook: How long should a co-creation session run? I suggest that you plan for 1.5 to 2 hours. Allow people to focus within this defined period of time. Make it effective and finish punctually. Review the day's progress, and define clear action steps.

Visualise Complexity

When we deal with complexity, visualising the current state is a great starting point to bring people together to set the foundation for simplification.

However, in the workplace, we are typically more familiar with using words or numbers in our communications. When was the last time you drew a picture? Perhaps with your children at home? Perhaps you doodle when you're on the phone? Or are you having a hard time recalling the last time you drew?

As toddlers, we started drawing before we were able to write, and we drew all the time. A few random scribbles were enough for us to visualise the imaginative world that we had in us, and to delight our parents. Drawing was part of playing, thinking and being. And we were very confident about our drawings.

As we grew older into school age, however, we began to judge our drawings. Some kids' drawings were better than ours, or vice versa. There were kids known for drawing well, and other kids shied away from drawing. The act of drawing slowly became a rather specialised activity for talented kids rather than something for everybody.

When we entered the workforce, we had to become "professional". This means we don't draw anymore. We use computer software like PowerPoint, Word or Excel. If we look at our typical office work, we have a lot of meetings, where we present our ideas or discuss problems. Then we may create another document and share it by email and have another meeting.

We talk, we write, we analyse, we present using words and numbers only.

The limitations of words and numbers

There is nothing wrong with using words or numbers. Both are very powerful elements of communication and problem-solving. However, there are limitations to using *only* words and numbers, especially when we are dealing with complexity.

- We may not get a full mental picture of a process, or we may not fully grasp the complexity of an issue.

- We may not see the connection between different parts of an issue if they are divided across pages, slides or spreadsheet columns.

- People in the room may not have the same understanding of the issue, because they may have interpreted the words and numbers differently and have built their own mental image. Just like when we read a description of a scene in a book, we create our own picture from the understanding, as opposed to seeing the scene in a movie.

This is when drawing a picture comes in handy. A picture can powerfully overcome the communication gap and instantly illuminate the complexity of an issue.

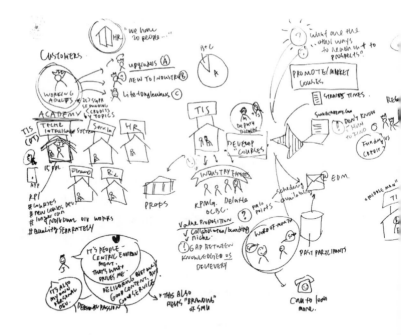

What do I mean by drawing a picture?

Here, by "drawing", I don't mean a technical drawing or a painting. All I mean is a freehand sketch, a sketch that consists of shapes, arrows, and stick men. It is often known as "visual facilitation", the idea being that you draw simple pictures "live" as a discussion unfolds. The process consists of asking questions, the subject matter experts answering the questions, and the visual facilitator representing the ideas in graphic form.

How drawing helps in understanding complexity

1. Giving a PowerPoint presentation is a one-way communication; drawing during a meeting is interactive. Hand-drawn pictures have a soft power in inviting people to a discussion. When we start sketching an idea out on a whiteboard, people immediately pay attention to what's going to unfold.

2. Simple drawings succinctly capture an idea or data point in a visual element. And these visual elements add up to the big picture.

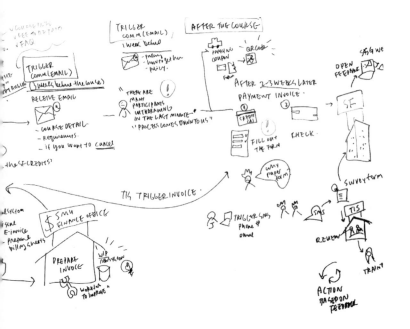

3. As the picture builds up, it allows people to clarify certain issues, to understand the connections. I often notice during visual facilitation sessions that people realise at this point that their understanding of, say, a process was quite different from that of people in other divisions.

4. This realisation is powerful, and it helps the group to build a common understanding of the discussed process or issue.

5. Once the picture is complete, the team can move on to identify pain points, or potential areas for innovation, or any other conclusions that matter to the project.

6. By the time the team members walk out of the room, it is certain that everyone has the same big picture in their heads. There is no longer the problem of gross misunderstandings or misinterpretation, as the issue's complexity has been thoroughly visualised and clarified.

How to facilitate visually

Visual facilitation is not hard to learn, yet it pays enormous dividends. You need four things to get started. These are: (1) a visual vocabulary; (2) a whiteboard; (3) people; (4) and a set of questions.

Visual vocabulary

A visual vocabulary is a set of simple graphical symbols that you will use to make your drawings. It works in the same way that a vocabulary of words allows you form sentences and convey meaning. This is my visual vocabulary:

Having visualised so many internal processes and customer experiences, I've found that I need only this handful of elements to visualise even the most complex processes:

1. **People,** e.g. customers, internal roles
2. **Touchpoints,** e.g. website, app, brochure, calls, email
3. **Parties involved,** e.g. internal departments, external agencies
4. **Basic shapes** to connect, emphasise, identify pain points

Develop your own visual vocabulary, one that is relevant to your business context.

Whiteboard and markers

A whiteboard lets you draw, erase and redraw all very quickly and spontaneously. If you don't have a whiteboard, you can use any large wall space and a long roll of paper instead. Markers in an assortment of colours – to represent different categories of information – are essential. For example, you could use black to sketch out the process, red for pain points, and green for potential ideas.

People

You need to bring the right people into the room. For example, if your goal is to understand the current auditing process to identify digital transformation opportunities, you will need **users of the process** and **experts** such as auditors. You will need project team **members** so that they get to ask questions, clarify and understand the current process that people are dealing with. The users of the process can be **customers** if the project scope deals with customers' process or journey.

Questions and structure

Successful visual facilitation depends on **asking the right questions and having a mindset of curiosity and inquiry.** I strongly recommend structuring your questions in a way that leads the participants to think through the issues step by step. Let's take a look at an example:

1. **Articulate today's goal:** "Today we would like to understand the current audit process. I'm going to facilitate and visually describe the process based on the conversations we have. It will take about an hour, and then we'll use another 30 minutes to discuss where our opportunities lie in digitising our services."

2. **Define the users of the process:**
   Who are the people involved?
   What are their goals?
   Is there anyone else involved in this process, internally or externally?

3. **Identify the start of the process:**
   How does this process begin?
   Who initiates this?
   How do customers first hear about this?

4. **Follow through the process in as much detail as possible:**
   What happens next?
   Where does this information go?
   What channels are used?
   How long does it take?
   Who is responsible for this action?
   What's the relationship between these two divisions?
   How frequently do they interact with each other?

5. **Define the end of the process:**
   When does this process end?
   Does anything else happen after this?

6. **Debrief and conclusion for today:**
   What surprised you after seeing this picture?
   What was interesting?
   Where are the pain points we need to address?
   What are the areas we need to dig deeper and research further?
   Where are the areas for opportunities?

7. **Thank the participants and define next steps.**

Visual facilitation is one of the most useful tools at the beginning of a project. It helps us understand the "as is" status and the complexity of the problem. Embracing and understanding complexity is the start of the simplicity process. Use visual facilitation to make this process clear and enjoyable for your team.

Concretise the abstract through prototyping

If a picture is worth 1000 words, a prototype
is worth 1000 meetings.
— David Kelly, founder of IDEO

The concept of prototyping originates from the world of product design and engineering. The purpose was to build a sample, model, or version of a product to test a concept or process.[4]

When I introduced the concept of prototyping to one of the project teams at a bank's wealth management division, it was a foreign concept to them. "Isn't this a designer or engineer's tool? Don't we need special equipment or software to build a prototype?"

However, prototyping is not exclusively a designer's or engineer's tool. It is a very useful thinking tool for everyone, especially when dealing with so-called "wicked problems", where the problems are unclear and the environment is uncertain.

A bank founded by 9-year-old

One day I took my 9-year-old daughter to a bank branch.

"Sabina, from now on, instead of giving you your pocket money in cash, I will put it into this card. You can use this card to pay at shops or take money out from this machine. All you need to carry is this card."

I was very mindful of not using banking terms such as "deposit" or "withdraw" when I introduced the ATM to her.

Her eyes beamed. And she wanted to use it immediately.

"I would like to put this money into my card," she said as she pulled $6.50 out of her pocket.

"Oh, sorry," I said. "I forgot to tell you that you can't put coins into the machine. It has to be over $10."

"Sigh. Okay, then can I take money out from the card?"

"Sure you can," I replied happily, as I showed her how to insert the card into the machine. "How much would you like to take out?"

"Twelve dollars."

There was a short pause from myself, as again I realised I had not explained all the aspects of ATMs.

"Oh, sorry. I forgot to tell you that the amount needs to be in round numbers, like $10, $20 or $30."

Sabina sighed again. I asked her if she would like to withdraw $20 instead of $12, but she said no. She felt $20 was too much money to carry around, given that her allowance was $6 a week.

So that was the end of my attempt to introduce her to bank cards and ATMs. We left without having made any deposit or withdrawal. Using an ATM was not as straightforward or obvious as I had thought.

After we got home, Sabina disappeared into her room to do her own thing. When I looked in on her a few hours later, I found her busy making something. She had created her own ATM machine out of a carton box!

It looked a lot like a real ATM. It had a dial pad drawn in black marker, and a card slot cut into the side.

Sabina then showed me all the exciting features of her ATM. "Now I can put all my coins into this bank!" she said as she proudly pointed to the slot for coins, which perfectly solved the problem she had faced earlier that day. The coins that she put into the slot dropped into a tray she had installed inside the box; if she wanted to withdraw any coins, she just needed to lift the flap of the box, which immediately pulled out the tray of coins. The sides of the ATM had other interesting functions, such as one for "weekly savings", which reflected her financial principles and desire to save more.

From that day, this carton ATM became her primary banking system. She could withdraw and deposit money as often as she liked, and in the exact amounts she wanted, 24/7, right in her own room.

This is called "prototyping" – making ideas tangible.

As children, we used our hands to make things, to express our emotions, to devise solutions, just like Sabina did with her ATM. We all had this ability and desire to solve problems with our hands. Somehow, along the way, we lost it.

Value of prototyping

1. Ideas flourish in the act of making
In organisations, we tend to think and act in abstract terms. The secret to generating great ideas is to start *making* things instead of mulling endlessly over strategic concepts. **Our hands and brains are interconnected; as you move your hands, your brain starts to generate ideas more effectively.**

I've seen this magic happen over and over again. When I encourage project teams or executive students to prototype their ideas – whether it's a new strategy, product or idea – in the beginning people hesitate. They feel the idea is not clear enough yet to make something out of it. But as they start stretching out, or mocking something up, slowly but surely the energy changes. Ideas take shape, discussions become more passionate, and people get truly excited about the possibilities they have unlocked.

"How did you feel
before, during and after prototyping?"

 D

Before: Uncertain
During: Excited, Inspired, Hopeful
After: Empowered, more Inspired than before.

The power of role playing and beauty of highlighting emotions.

 J

Before- I felt unsure and nervous as I m not as creative as I would hoped to be.

During- can be awkward when you and ur teammates are not on the same page. But u learn to compromise and try different ways. More ideas were generated as we moved along.

After- Felt awesome to see a prototype. It was relatable and tangible.

*Managers' reflections on a
prototyping experience*

2. Prototyping allows us to test the concept with the users

Prototypes let us see what works and what doesn't in the early stages of development without having to invest a lot of resources. Prototyping doesn't have to be polished, or produced in a specific format. It can be a sketch on a piece of paper, things made out of a cardboard box, wireframes, or even a role-play. Apple's first mouse was prototyped using the ball from a roll-on deodorant and a plastic butter box.

When a prototype looks too polished, it becomes too precious – people are reluctant to tinker with it, to improve it further. Not only that, when it's too polished, users may think the design is almost done, and hold back their honest feedback.

Early concept prototypes for a financial app

Early concept prototypes for a financial literacy programme

Early testing increases the willingness to change

Testing early with the right level of prototype is crucial, because it also affects the willingness to change. The authors of *Sprint: How to Solve Big Problems and Test New Ideas in Just Five Days*[5] capture the importance of timing perfectly:

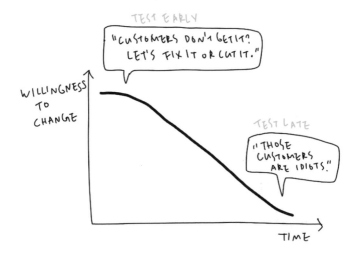

When an idea exists in a low-resolution prototype, it's really not a big deal to change. For example, one of the initial naming ideas we had for FRANK by OCBC was "Naked". The team thought it was cool, something different, and it connoted the idea of transparency. However, when we took the name to the prototype store and exposed it to the target audience, we knew immediately it didn't work. So we killed it.

3. Prototyping creates a shared vision among diverse stakeholders

An idea becomes really powerful when people can see it and touch it. Often, a lot of potentially great ideas are trapped inside Power-Point slides. By giving ideas concrete form, we can engage our stakeholders in shaping the vision together.

As shared in Chapter 3, to create a new brand like FRANK by OCBC, it was crucial to make the vision as tangible as possible. By prototyping the store, products and service model, we allowed all the stakeholders to see the same picture. If the concept had been presented only on a deck of slides, we wouldn't have gotten the kind of buy-in we needed to execute some of the more hard-to-visualise ideas.

Plus, prototyping can be fun to build. Using our hands and building something is one of the most underrated activities in the business world. When the environment is right, prototyping among stakeholders can boost collective creativity.

FRANK by OCBC 2.0 prototype

4. Prototyping builds a culture of experimentation

In today's fast-changing world, a spirit of experimentation is critical to staying agile and adaptive. Prototyping is one of the best tools to help companies create this culture. Its tangibility and visibility makes the ideation process especially productive, sparking new ideas towards simplicity.

How to prototype?

1. Start from the visible layers of experience
While complex experiences typically stem from the core of the Layers of Complexity – i.e. the product or topic itself being complex – the best way to start tackling complexity is to work from the outside-in. The outer layers are what users can see, such as the way content is written or the way the interface is designed.

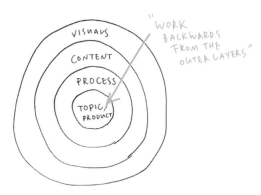

Why start from the outer layers? Isn't that avoiding the real source of complexity, you may wonder.

Say, if your team plans to simplify a complex financial product and the product experience, a good starting point is to prototype the product's brochure or web page. The point here isn't whether you produce a brochure or a website; **it is to envision how your customers will discover, understand and see your product.**

Strategic topics tend to be abstract. Think about your organisation's digital transformation agenda – can people in the organisation describe exactly what it is, and feel what the end-state is like? Particularly when dealing with strategic concepts, organisations will benefit from concretising these concepts in a user-facing touchpoint, such as a new product brochure.

What this does is to trigger questions that challenge us to reflect whether a product or process is easy to understand and perform, and force us to really look at how the content is perceived through our customers' eyes. This provides the foundation to work backwards from the users' encounter with our product.

2. Envision the end-state through prototyping

One of the complex experiences I had to simplify when working on an insurance project was the policy illustration document. This document contains tables of different scenarios such as how long and how much the insurance will cover, how long and how much customers need to pay, and how much customers can get (or lose) if they decide to surrender.

During the research, we found that most customers struggled to make sense of the rows and rows of numbers. The agents also had to work harder (and print stacks of pages) to prepare for meetings with customers and explain all the scenarios.

Simplifying the document seemed way overdue, but we learned that the template was determined not by the company, but by external regulators. This meant that to redesign it, we would need the approval of both internal and external parties.

What we did was to design a simplified policy illustration document that realistically imagined its future state. In this policy illustration prototype, the visual design was massively improved to provide the policy-holders a clear overview. The language was simplified, replacing jargon with everyday language, while important information as well as the place for signatures was enlarged and highlighted.

When the team took this to the external regulators to seek their approval, not only did the regulators approve it, they were inspired to change the default template to influence how other insurance companies produced these documents. After all, the regulators' job is to protect consumers, so they are very interested in achieving simplicity for the benefit of consumers.

If the meeting had happened without a visualisation of a possible future state, the answer from the regulators might have been a flat no. When we help people visualise a better future, that's when we can inspire and influence them.

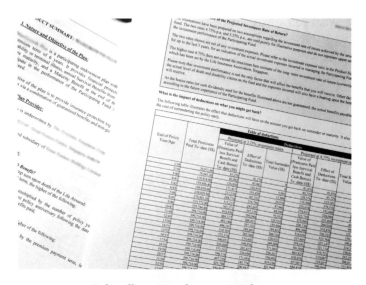

Policy illustration document: Before

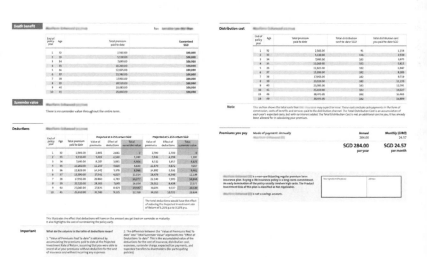

Policy illustration document: After

3. What you are designing is an experience, not technology

Always remember that prototyping is not fundamentally about technology, even though it sounds very high-tech. What we are designing is an experience.

In this prototype, the design team was envisioning the future of executive learning using virtual reality. They created a scenario of a busy working mother. She wants to invest in herself, but has no time for it. Having to spend most of her day at home taking her of her kids, she cannot pursue what she wants to learn as a professional. The team acted out this scenario, and showed how their proposed VR solution would fit into the working mother's busy life, empowering her to use her limited free time to engage in rich learning experiences.

Here, there was no high technology involved in creating the prototype, just good old cardboard and role-play. But when the idea was shared with stakeholders using this highly relatable scenario, it immediately opened up the discussion about how technology could then be used to enable the experience that the team had painted.

4. Don't fall in love with your prototypes. Iterate, iterate and iterate

Prototyping new ideas can be energising, but don't fall in love with your ideas just yet. One of the traps many companies fall into in adopting design thinking is to run each activity only once and to implement right away based on the first round of research and prototyping.

Based on my experience, the first round of insights and prototyping never produces a great outcome even if you feel very excited about it. The number of iterations it takes to reveal valuable insights that get acted on is three rounds at the minimum (this is from my personal experience), even for a very small project. If the project is big and complex, the number of iterations can go up to two or three digits.

Throughout these repeated iterations, we need to have a mindset of humility. What we learned is great, but we might not be there yet in identifying the best way to solve the problem. Continue to test, learn and prototype again, stripping off layer after layer of complexity, until you reach the level of simplicity that brings joy to customers.

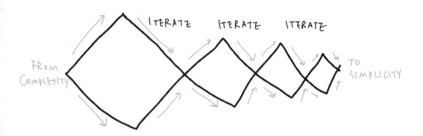

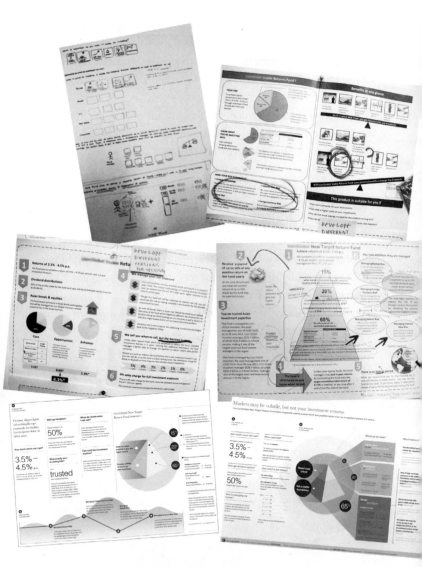

An example how prototypes evolve through many rounds of iterations

Be a pain sponge

The simplicity curve

When I am in the midst of a simplification process, I often get this feeling that the team has wandered into a massive forest of complexity, and whatever we do seems to complicate the project more and more.

This feeling comes about because in the process of simplification, we need to dissect the subject matter, examine various scenarios, evaluate options and consider all the implications. It also involves prototyping and testing options in order to simplify the right things. And lots of other things may be thrown your way. The project scope may be broadened. You may need to amass more knowledge. You may need to seek external stakeholders' approval. So as you start a project, the goal might be simple, but in order to achieve it, you will inevitably have to go through the "hump" of complexity.

A gift from my boss

One late evening in my office, I was probably at the peak of this complexity hump, buried in a pile of documents and prototypes. I was working on simplifying a form, and was looking at prototype version 4, trying to find the best way to arrange the information on the form. But whatever solution I tried, I felt as though I was complicating it, not simplifying it.

I sighed and let my frustration out. Just at that moment, my boss passed by my desk on his way out of the office. He tapped my shoulder and said: "Jin, just soak up the pain."

The next morning, when I arrived in the office, I saw something on my table. It was a "gift" from my boss: a sponge, a pain sponge.

The pain sponge became our team's mascot. We each had our own pain sponge on our desk to remind ourselves what it takes to design a simple customer experience. Simplicity doesn't happen by accident; it is only achieved through hard work. We called it "absorbing the pain".

But the pain was worth it. We knew that we were absorbing the pain on behalf of the future users of the form. The goal of those rounds and rounds of prototyping was to eliminate as many pain points for users as possible.

Removing pain points requires a broad range of painful activities, including: challenging the status quo; convincing people who have countless reasons not to change the way things are; spending hours and days defining what can be removed; having long discussions with legal and compliance officers; pushing the boundaries of how the customer experience can be simplified and designed for delight.

The more pain the working team soaks up now, the less pain for the thousands or even millions of eventual users out there, and therefore a more delightful experience for them. How much pain are you absorbing in order to reduce your users' pain?

YOU =
PAIN SPONGE

CUSTOMERS' PAIN

THE MORE PAIN YOU SOAK UP,
THE SIMPLER YOUR CUSTOMER
EXPERIENCE WILL BE.

So whenever you feel daunted by the complexity and amount of work ahead of you, remind yourself that you are totally on the right track being the pain sponge. Going through the hump is part of the process of reaching simplicity. Be a pain sponge – that's the mindset that organisations need in order to drive simplicity.

Chapter 5
Focus

MORE

LESS BUT
BETTER

Focus, time and money are our three most important resources... Focus, however, is little understood, although today it's the most valuable of these three resources, the most crucial to our success and our well-being.
— Rolf Dobelli[1]

IN MY WORKSHOPS and executive classes, there is a ritual I carry out, which I do not enjoy very much, and certainly neither do the participants, and that is confiscating everybody's mobile phones – and sometimes laptops too!

At the start of class, I introduce the rule and go around taking people's phones and putting them in a box (which I call "The phone box to focus"). I sense all sort of emotions from the participants, who are usually senior leaders of their organisations. Shock. Anger. Despair. But since everybody is doing it, people are cooperative despite their discomfort at not being able to access their devices during the workshop.

The moment the phones are taken away, I sense a new feeling: a fresh gust of attention. Attention is obviously invisible, but the attention I get right after the devices are taken away is so intense and palpable. I do believe this energy is precious and can make all the difference.

I've found that running workshops or meetings without devices yields amazing results. It allows people to immerse themselves fully in the topic of discussion. The energy level is high, people are engaged, and they often have fun as well. Fun fact: Some of these executive students become so excited about the distraction-free experience that they go back and implement it in their own companies!

The work of simplicity is cognitively demanding. If we allow ourselves to be constantly distracted, given the time it takes to get back to our tasks, it's almost like we are setting ourselves up for failure. Researchers at the University of California found that it takes an average of 23 minutes for distracted workers to return to their tasks. The cost of fragmented attention is more than a third of an hour!

In this time of great complexity and distractions, we need focus more than ever. Focus is not just a mental state; it is an asset – an asset that we need to defend, manage and learn. When we focus on doing fewer but better things, we show our customers that we value their time. **When you offer customers focus, in return you earn their trust.**

In this chapter, I will introduce steps and tools to identify what matters for your business and for your customers, and how to craft a focused value proposition.

In this chapter

FOMO and comprehensiveness

Fear of missing out (FOMO) refers to the anxiety that other people are having rewarding experiences from which one is absent.[2] We often use FOMO to describe the feeling we get when we are constantly online, looking at the Instagram photos of friends, celebrities and strangers, and obsessed with what they are doing – and comparing that to our own lives.

However, I have observed that FOMO is pervasive in our work environment too. We are obsessed with what others – competitors and disruptors – are doing. While it is vital to scan the environment and adapt ourselves to stay competitive, we need to be mindful that FOMO can result in needless complexity, which harms our customer experience as well as our competitive advantage.

Side-effects of FOMO

One of the side-effects of FOMO is adding more things. If a competitor launches a credit card targeted at active travellers, we feel obliged to develop one too. Our new app might have launched with essential features presented in a clean interface, but as new features get tacked on with insufficient thought, it becomes cluttered and complicated.

Complexity is the nature of our business. That's why it's imperative to increase our sensitivity towards evolving complexity and to know how to change the current before it goes too complicated and gets in our way.

Adding more can hurt customer experience.

During a project simplifying a bank's corporate website, I was stunned by the sheer number of products (e.g. account types) that had to be presented. As the project unfolded, I learned that this was because product managers had been tasked to develop more products as their innovation KPI.

During the customer research, however, we discovered that having many products didn't help customers choose the account that was right for them. No matter how great your individual products are, an overly large number of products can hurt the overall customer experience.

The more choices people have, the harder it is for them to choose. This is called the Paradox of Choice, a theory formulated by the American psychologist Barry Schwartz. His research found that streamlining or eliminating consumer choices can greatly reduce their anxiety.[3] So why do we continue to think that *more* is better?

Comprehensiveness vs Simplicity

One of the reasons why it is hard to simplify systems or documents is because we tend to go for "comprehensiveness".

For one, we don't want to miss out on requirements coming from the legal and compliance departments. And we often believe that it is important to state everything, no matter how lengthy that is. When I look at an investment form that was designed in 2008 as a response to the global financial crisis, it is evident that we had to ask more questions in the form and state more terms and conditions to meet the legal and compliance requirements as a way to protect the bank (provided the customers understood all of them).

We also want to be comprehensive in meeting requirements from different users and stakeholders. We don't want to leave anyone out. Behind a healthcare company's complex intranet system jammed with boxes of information, I found that the intranet was treated as "real estate" by the various business heads such as corporate communications, marketing, products, operations, technology, human resources, research and development, finance, etc. In order to make everyone happy, the intranet system was designed to provide space for each business unit to fill with information they wanted to say.

In dealing with massive amounts of information and requirements, the temptation is to be as comprehensive as possible. While being comprehensive is important, in order to achieve simplicity, we need to be able to make certain "trade-offs" based on priority.

If a form is meant to help customers make a confident investment decision, we need to trade off the comprehensive lengthy terms and conditions in legalese for a concise summary that highlights the implications in plain language. Legal professionals will certainly argue that by doing so, the clause may not cover all possible scenarios, but through a thorough examination of the matter and its implications, you may need to trade off perfection for practical simplicity.

If improving employee productivity by changing the intranet system is the priority, we should be willing to trade off the comprehensiveness of information provided by all the business units for curated time-sensitive information that matters to employees.

Edward de Bono argues that this sort of trade-off requires a clear sense of values and priorities. Since it is usually not possible to have everything, there has to be a choice between different values. It is important to be deliberate and conscious about the choices that are being made.[4]

When I was working on a digital wealth management platform, we made the bold decision to significantly reduce the number of products we offered (75% less than what the bank's competitors were offering then). It was a conscious trade-off between making it comprehensive (offering every single product we had) and helping customers build confidence in investing (offering fewer but better products).

Adding more is easy. If feels safer to say more than less.

Adding more is lazy. Because you don't need to examine the implications and take responsibility for the decision.

In all the complex forms, communication materials, processes, websites, systems I've worked with, the primary reason for having too much info, too many features, was that the owners of the content or process were not challenging the status quo in order to pursue what really matters.

Innovation doesn't end at creating more and more better products. The job is done only when we also eliminate things that are no longer relevant, and ensure that the launching of the new product enhances the overall experience.

Ask questions to focus

*While there are many "answer" books available ... we must
figure out our own solutions and answers to the complex,
individualised challenges we face in work and in our
personal life. ... That tool is the humble question.*
— Warren Berger [5]

How do we learn to focus in today's complex business environment? I've been searching for so-called experts' methods to help businesses identify where to focus, but there don't seem to be many methods available. And in the workshops, meetings and sprints carried out in my simplicity work, it was not a bunch of frameworks that guided my project teams to focus.

What guided us to focus was a set of basic questions.

In Chapter 3, we discussed how asking open-ended questions during customer research helps us dig deeper into consumers' minds. In the same way, asking questions is a simple but most powerful tool for probing what matters to your business and your customers, and thus finding the most relevant focus.

To identify your focus, ask yourself the following questions:

1. **Your customers' why**
   What jobs are they trying to get done?

2. **Your business's why**
   Why are you doing this? (purpose)

3. **Your focus**
   Who are you designing for?
   What problem do you want to solve?
   What's the one thing that differentiates you?

Your focus lies in the overlap between what matters most to consumers and where your business can create the most value.

Having a clear answer to these questions won't be easy. It takes a whole project team, stakeholders and decision-makers, and requires many rounds of discussion and adaptation. Also, given that launching a project takes a long time (from a few months to a few years, depending on the complexity), it is vital to ask yourself these questions, for the answers will be the team's North Star when the temptation to add more features arises.

Your customers' why

Customers' why refer to their needs, motivation and aspirations. You might have heard this expression: "People don't want a drill, they want a hole." The reason why people buy a drill is to make a hole, and they want to make a hole to do something – hang a picture on the wall, or make a drainage hole for a potted plant.

What jobs are your customers trying to get done?

When it comes to simplifying customer experience or designing a digital product, identifying your customers' deeper needs, motivation and aspirations is not as simple as just asking them. More often than not, they themselves aren't able to articulate what drives their decision to buy a particular product or brand.

The "jobs to be done" theory (JTBD) developed by Clayton Christensen posits that we should be looking at buying decisions as "hiring" decisions instead.[6] The question we should be asking ourselves is: **"What jobs are customers trying to get done by hiring our products or services?"** instead of "What do customers want?" This switch of questioning can immediately shine a new light into customers' minds.

Let's have a look at some examples.

Why do people hire milkshakes?

Years ago, McDonald's wanted to find a way to boost its milkshake sales.

First, they identified target customers and asked them questions about "how to improve the milkshakes". Based on the feedback and suggestions, McDonald's made improvements to their milkshakes, but it didn't have much impact on sales and profit.

That's when Clayton Christensen's team joined to apply JTBD to look at the business challenge differently. **Instead of asking**

people what they wanted from the milkshake, they sought to find out what people were trying to get done through buying a milkshake.

The first thing the team did was to spend 18 hours observing customers coming into the store. They paid close attention to circumstances such as who these customers were, what time they came, whether they bought milkshakes with other food, whether they wanted the milkshakes as takeaway or dine-in.

The most surprising observation was that most milkshakes were sold in the morning before 8:30am, and these buyers were mostly arriving alone, and buying only milkshakes. And then they drove off.

The team talked to the milkshake buyers to better understand their needs, motivations and context. It turned out that people were "hiring" milkshakes to accompany them on a long drive ahead. First of all, milkshakes are thick, so they won't spill easily in the car. More importantly, they take a good long time to consume (23 minutes to suck in through the thin straw).

The long-distance drivers and commuters reported that they had previously "hired" other things to perform the same JTBD. Some said they had hired a banana to do the job, but were disappointed that the banana was done within a minute. Some hired bagels, but spreading and eating cream cheese while driving was messy. Some hired doughnuts or Snickers, but felt guilty eating them.

With this insight, the McDonald's team had a clear focus. For this "morning job" (they also discovered a few other jobs during the research), they focused on improving the texture of the milkshakes so they stayed enjoyable for a longer time. They also created a seamless in-store experience for customers who were just there to buy milkshakes for their commute. The sales of milkshakes went up sevenfold.

JTBD helps innovators know where to focus and how to focus. The jobs that customers want done are out there, they already exist. By identifying the job, and refining your product to help customers do the job better, you can safely predict that customers will buy it.

Why did I hire iPod?

Back in 2001, when the iPod was first introduced, I remember being a proud owner of this new gadget. Despite my friends' scepticism about having to use Apple's music system iTunes, as opposed to freely downloading and uploading mp3 music to the device, my decision to buy an iPod was a no-brainer.

Why? Because it was cool. I loved the wheel-button, the feel of the shiny white plastic finish, the interplay of physical touch and digital display. Most of all, I loved wearing the white earphones that came with the iPod.

An electronic device in white, particularly earphones, was a rare offering at the time. While my iPod was usually tucked away in my pocket or my bag, wearing the white earphones was a visible signal to the world that I was part of the Apple tribe. I enjoyed the feeling of being one of the early adopters among a sea of black-earphone wearers. Occasionally I would encounter some-one else wearing the white earphones, and we would exchange a look of pride.

What was the job I wanted to get done by hiring the iPod? Cer-tainly I wanted to store music and listen on the go (functional). But I also wanted to look cool and feel cool (emotional), which was probably a bigger driver for me. And reflecting on my story, there was one more job: being part of a tribe (social).

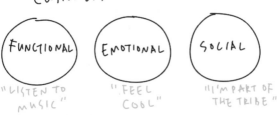

Every job has a functional, emotional, and social dimension. Understanding this can help us focus on what customers' problems we aim to solve.

Why do people hire a financial service?

When we use JTBD as a lens, we get to uncover new perspectives that often contradict the usual perceptions of a business. When I once conducted research to better understand the financial needs of professionals in their 30s, I learned some interesting "jobs" they were trying to get done.

Banks often position themselves as providers of financial knowledge, products and advisory services. However, the professionals we spoke to had other jobs which were not being addressed:

What banks think customers want	Jobs that customers want to get done
Getting financial advice from the bank	Ticking off important milestones such as starting a family, buying a car
Getting an investment strategy from the bank	Making a sound investment decision with my own sources of trust (which may include banks)

This understanding of customers' real jobs shifts the business's perspective. From there, companies can focus on how to create experiences customers need to get their jobs done well.

How to identify JTBD

The best way to identify JTBD is through direct contact with your customers. Observing and talking to people, like the way the team at McDonald's did, is a great way to start. This is in line with the research methods introduced in Chapter 3. Empathising with customers is the key to understanding their JTBD.

But if you asked a customer, "What job were you trying to get done?", you probably wouldn't get a helpful answer, because people rarely think that way, and often the decision to buy (or hire) a product or service happens at the subconscious level and is heavily influenced by the context.

Instead, ask them to tell you their story. Why did they feel the need for something? What kind of journey did they go through? How did they feel along the way? Stories are rich sources of information because they incorporate telling details such as time, situation, environment, circumstances, emotional state.

Here are some very effective questions to help you capture stories from people that will reveal their JTBD:

- **Motivation and context**
  Tell me your recent experience with this kind of situation?
  What triggered your thoughts of buying this kind of product?
  What was happening in your life around that time?

- **Functional**
  What information were you searching for? And where?
  What features were important to you? And why?
  How long did it take?
  What did you do after the purchase?

- **Emotional**
  How did the process make you feel?
  How did you feel when the product arrived?

- **Social**
  Who helped you make the decision?
  Who did you talk to about the product after buying it?
  What did your friends and family say about it?

Your business's why

Let's now turn to your business's why – the purpose of your business, the intent of your brand or product, the very reason for your business's existence. Alongside your customers' why, this is the second area that focus comes from.

Simon Sinek, in one of the most-watched TED talks of all time, shares the Golden Circle, his discovery of how successful leaders inspire people. The Golden Circle represents **Why** (a sense of purpose), **How** (methods or process) and **What** (results such as products).[7]

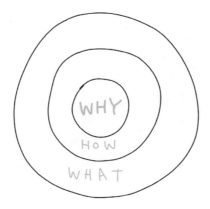

While this model was discovered in the context of leadership and communication, I've found it powerful in articulating a business's purpose and translating that into how to design experiences and products.

Articulating business "why" drives focused innovation.

From the birth of FRANK by OCBC in 2011, the brand has been continuously evolving. Internally it was referred to as FRANK 2.0 and 3.0. Each launch had its own themes as customers matured in their personal and professional lives, and as the wider environment changed.

But what I find most remarkable is **the clarity of its purpose and the consistency of its brand personality** throughout all these years. What guided the team was a relentless focus on the vision of creating a stylish, simple and meaningful bank for millennials. When the why of the business was clearly defined, even as external forces changed the market and consumer behaviour, we were able to adapt our approach (the what, and the how). FRANK by OCBC has evolved through 2.0 and 3.0 having this clear why at the heart.

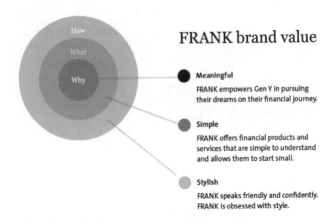

FRANK brand value

Meaningful
FRANK empowers Gen Y in pursuing their dreams on their financial journey.

Simple
FRANK offers financial products and services that are simple to understand and allows them to start small.

Stylish
FRANK speaks friendly and confidently. FRANK is obsessed with style.

FRANK 2.0: Empowering millennials through content

With FRANK 2.0, one of the key strategies for further sharpening brand value was to build customers' financial literacy. "Content" had to become the new currency for the bank. Content here refers to genuine pieces of advice, tools, tips, stories – basically anything that is not marketing communications or hidden information.

One of the daring changes we made was in communicating the implications of late credit card payments. Typically, information on charges and fees is found in fine print, away from the main page of the card statement, and reads like this:

policy, in the event we do not receive from you the minimum payment amount due on your statement of account by the relevant payment due date, you will be in default. If you have three or more defaults and/or one default which remains unpaid for two or more consecutive months in the last 12 months, we may adjust the interest rate applicable to your Card Account from prevailing interest rate to 29.99% p.a (subject to compounding). This higher interest rate will be in effect for 12 consecutive months. During this period, if you maintain a good credit record and your Card Account is not cancelled or terminated, your interest rate may be reinstated to our prevailing base interest rate.

But what if we could help customers build their financial literacy by visualising the consequences of not paying their credit card bills on time? What is the financial impact if someone doesn't pay for two months, or three months, in a row? When we visualised it as a set of bar graphs, I was shocked at how quickly the amount of debt increases!

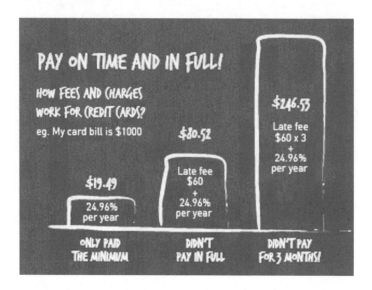

This idea was not welcomed by some stakeholders because it's not how a bank usually communicates, and frankly this is how companies make money.

But by focusing on the brand's why – empowering millennials in their financial journey – the team was able to successfully challenge the status quo, and bring the stakeholders round to make the right decision in delivering the desired experience for the brand's customers.

FRANK 3.0: Empowering millennials through providing a platform for passion

In 2018, the team began to face a new wave of change. In a country where some 18-year-olds are making thousands a day running e-commerce stores, where 9-to-5 jobs are frowned upon by youths, and the ultimate luxury is the freedom to do what you want, when you want, and Instagram it for all to see – where does a financial brand for youths fit in?

Based on conversations with this target market, the team saw that FRANK would need to adapt and evolve, **to empower youths to thrive in this new world of the gig economy.**

Crucially, the team learned that a key driver behind the gig economy is passion. This translated to pivoting the brand's content away from exclusively financial knowledge to include real-life stories that millennials can relate to. The new content not only offered inspiration and practical tips, but ultimately led to the brand becoming a platform for its users to follow and share their passions.

For example, we were interested in telling the story of Joanne Lim, a graphic-designer-turned-entrepreneur.[8] While travelling in New York City, she fell in love with the art of calligraphy, and when she returned to Singapore from her holiday, she felt the computer was cold compared to the tactility of calligraphy, and so decided to start her own calligraphy business. Joanne's story attracted a group of people who shared the same passion. Her story and her work formed a community.

What products or experiences could FRANK offer to empower youths to follow their passion? Out of this question, the team created a broad range of novel ideas, from workshops and customisable card designs to new financial products.

How a passion became a product

The FRANK branches, which were initially designed to be "retail stores" for customers to "shop" for stylish financial products, were redesigned. We repositioned them as places for youths to meet, conduct workshops, share knowledge, find others with similar interests. In an age where everything is going digital, I believe physical spaces still provide some of the best opportunities for building human connections and growing the community.

Prototype of a FRANK branch as a platform for passion

The result of focused innovation

The results speak for themselves. FRANK customers have a "stickier" relationship with the bank than customers who didn't experience the brand. And this is true for all the key measures that matter to the business, such as assets under management, credit card spending, number of products, and whether customers are using the bank as their primary bank.

Another kind of result I personally value is how people are enjoying the brand. Customers inside FRANK stores are regularly seen having fun and taking selfies with the products on display. A blogger created a fun series of images using the card design postcards. Emotionally engaged customers become loyal to the brand. This is one of the most rewarding outcomes of putting customers at the centre of your focus.

The sweet spot: Where can you create the most value?

Once you have identified (1) the customers' jobs and (2) your business's why, it's time to look for the overlap – the sweet spot for your focus. Here are 3 questions to help your team identify the sweet spot where your business can create the most value.

1. Who are you designing for?

In the kick-off meeting for a new project, one of the first questions I ask the project team is: "Who are we designing this for?"

The most common answer I get is: "It's for everyone." And they give me a look that implies I've asked a silly question. It's true that we are designing for everyone in a way, particularly if your products or services are intended for the masses. However, in order to create a product or service that delivers a simply delightful experience, you must establish a clear picture of who exactly you are designing for.

Design for specific people, not a generic creature

At the start of the design process for a digital wealth management platform for OCBC Bank, a specific target group was not determined. The imagined users included everyone who was already investing, or planning to invest. The business lead was understandably interested in meeting as many people's needs as possible, to increase the user base. The project team thus reached out to a broad range of people, ranging from their early 20s to late 50s, with varying investment experience.

As the research unfolded, the team picked up some very interesting behaviour from a particular group: people who did not necessarily have much investment experience, but who had a strong appetite for becoming more financially savvy. They were mostly in the active stages of their career and family-building. Despite being time-poor, they were actively seeking information, for example through participating in online investment groups. They were typically underserved by banks, and had not yet established a strong relationship with a specific banker or bank.

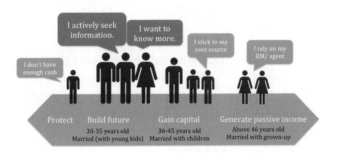

The team spotted an opportunity. Observing how this group of people sought information, hearing what their life aspirations were and how they felt about their current financial situation, the team started to form a clearer picture of who the primary target of the new digital service should be.

By zooming in on this primary target, the team was no longer designing for the generic "everyone". Their customer was now vivid and specific. Beyond the common needs shared by all kinds of users, there were situations where the needs of the target group were distinctively different.

For example, the target group was different from the savvy investors who already had their trusted sources of ideas and avenues of execution. The team designed the overall flow to be optimised for this less experienced target group, simplifying each step to help them manage the process better. **Such design decisions are not about excluding other groups of users; they're about fully understanding the implications, weighing the priorities, and making a conscious choice.**

Within three months of the launch, more than 60% of the users bought an investment online for the first time. Around 70% of users were under 40 years old, compared to less than 20% at branches. The result was unmistakable evidence that the target users who were underserved welcomed this digital solution.

2. What's the problem we want to solve?

From the customers' jobs you identified through the lens of JTBD, you can choose to tackle certain jobs as a strategy and to deliver a better experience than anyone else. For this digital wealth management project, we identified many jobs that customers were trying to get done, such as getting information, validating their decisions, buying investment products, managing investments, just to name a few. As the team prototyped and continued to test the concept with the target audience, it became clearer that **the problem we wanted to solve was to address the "lack of confidence" in people who are relatively new to investments.**

3. What's the one thing that differentiates you?

From there, we went further to discuss what was our unique selling point – in other words, the one thing that differentiated us. We analysed our competitors' offerings, and found that their weakest area was providing customers with support when it came to making decisions to sell their investments.

Putting it together in a focus statement

Having answered all the questions, it's time to put everything together in what I call a "focus statement", because above all, it helps internal teams to clarify purpose, targets and unique selling points. Here is a focus statement template:

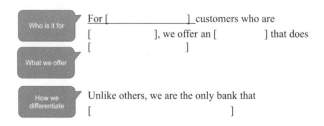

Who is it for

For [   ] customers who are
[   ], we offer an [   ] that does
[   ]

What we offer

How we differentiate

Unlike others, we are the only bank that
[   ]

It looks simple, but you will soon realise that it is not easy to condense ideas into these two sentences. It takes hard thinking and many rounds of iterations.

Take a look at version 0.7 of a project:

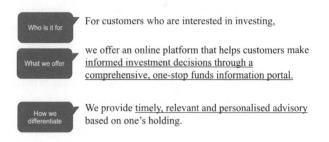

Here, you can see the team has carefully chosen words that describe the intent of the new service. Yet this version still includes a lot of big words such as "comprehensive", "one-stop shop", "timely", "personalised", etc. Distilling ideas to their essence is tough, and we often feel safer using many adjectives instead of fewer. This is a normal process towards simplification. The key is to go through this process and keep tightening your focus.

After many rounds of iterations, the final focus statement for the project evolved into this:

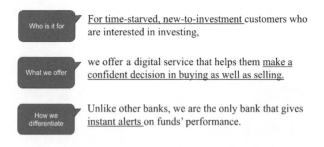

Right away you'll notice that this version has a more specific description of the target group, and a more succinct and concrete choice of words in defining the unique selling point.

This focus statement sharpened our focus, and helped to constantly remind us what was most important when difficult decisions had to be made.

Your focus statement is not your marketing pitch.

The focus statement was adapted from the "elevator pitch" developed by Geoffrey Moore, initially intended as a marketing pitch.[9] However, in the context of innovation projects, the focus statement is not the same as your marketing pitch, and you shouldn't approach it like a marketing pitch. If you do, you'll find you tend to use "big words" (see examples in Chapter 6.2) that appear to be sophisticated but are vague and unhelpful. The purpose of focus statements is to uncover and sharpen your focus among internal teams by using *real words* as a thinking tool.

Focus means doing fewer thing fabulously.

Take a rigorous approach in defining focus. A set of questions is the most powerful tool I've encountered. Use the set of basic questions introduced in this chapter to identify the sweet spot where you can add most value instead of doing more. This will take time and require hard decisions among your stakeholders, but competitive advantage lies in doing fewer things but better than anyone else.

Chapter 6
Speak human

AUTOMATE   HUMANISE

Clutter and confusion are failures of design,
not attributes of information.
— Edward Tufte

IT'S A COMMON MISTAKE. Companies spend a lot of time and money to build a nice website or app, but neglect other important touchpoints, like letters, forms, terms and conditions, or even "minor" things like website error messages that are left to the system default. These are actually great opportunities for humanising the customer experience and developing a positive relationship with your customers.

When I was involved in simplifying the letters produced by a bank, I personally reviewed over thousands of different templates to identify and analyse problems. While these templates varied in their objectives, ranging from operations to marketing, I quickly spotted a common problem. The letters all spoke as if the bank was a combination between a lawyer, a banker and a robot, even though they had been written by real human beings.

On top of improving the letters' tone of voice, the project team was tasked with digitising the correspondence process by adopting a new content management system, as opposed to using Word templates which were stored in different places. We needed a big change management effort at all levels, and decided that **instead of getting carried away by "digitising" the process, the team would focus on "humanising" the process by establishing a new editorial standard for the letters, as well as empowering letter writers**.

As part of this effort, my colleague Jordan Ng ran an interesting experiment. He took one of the existing letters, which asked customers to take an investment decision (see Chapter 6.2), and presented it to 10 customers for their action. It turned out that only 2 out of the 10 customers knew what to do – because they'd dealt with this kind of letter before. Three customers weren't very sure what to do and said they would ignore the letter. The remaining five customers said they wouldn't ignore it even though they didn't fully understand it, because the letter looked important, given it had dates, figures and a scissor line that called for action. So Jordan asked them what they would do? Their answer was: "I'd call the contact centre to clarify."

The interesting lesson was the "cost" of an unclear letter such as this. Contact centres are not the solution to unclear communications, because we learned that at the time of the project it cost the bank $7 every time a customer called. And this letter was supposed to be sent out to about half a million customers. What if half of them (250,000 customers) had problems knowing what to do? What if half of these people who didn't understand the letter (125,000 customers) decided to call the contact centre to clarify? The cost of an unclear letter might have been 125,000 customers x $7 = $875,000!

While this was a hypothetical estimation, the experiment was eye-opening for the letter writers. They saw how critical it was for a letter to be clear and simple. When companies communicate in jargon or robotic tones, not only does it hinder customers from understanding the message, it can also cost the company.

In this chapter, we will discuss how humanising communications simplifies the experience, and discuss tips on how to simplify different types of communications, from chatbots to legalese.

In this chapter

6.1 Human conversations make it simple
6.2 10 commandments of speaking human
6.3 Tell stories to connect
6.4 Bring your personality
6.5 How to humanise a chatbot
6.6 Simplifying legalese

Human conversations make it simple

Recall an incident when you had to do a very complex task, such as buying a home. There were many processes and people you had to deal with, such as a property agent, developer or house owner, architect, notary, banker. When I bought my apartment, it was a new construction project, and the process was even more complicated as it involved the authorities, who had to approve the building specs and floor plans. I spent days going through all the legal documents and mortgage contracts, and still felt deep in the swamp of complexity.

But when I met human beings like the notary and my banker, the complexity turned into comprehensible concepts. I sat down with each of them individually, and everything became clearer. I felt assured of what I needed to know and what I had to do. They didn't do anything spectacular, really; they just did a very competent, professional job. I couldn't help but wonder why I had struggled so much with those documents, which were essentially telling me the same thing.

What were the magic ingredients in the short meetings I had with them that simplified the complex process?

1. Firstly, they both possessed subject matter **knowledge**, and were therefore able to explain it to me clearly.

2. Secondly, they acted as a **pain sponge** (discussed in Chapter 4.7), soaking up all the complexity, and leaving me with **clarity**.

3. The third ingredient, which is the topic of this chapter, was the **human conversation**.

Human conversation, as opposed to the language of legal contracts, business reports or academic writing, goes straight to the heart. When we have a conversation, we use simple, everyday language rather than big words. We exchange questions and answers. We may look at materials together and discuss. We address the topic from the listener's point of view. We build a connection.

These elements of human conversation are the secret to simplifying complex communications of all kinds. If those documents that gave me so much grief had been able to "speak human", the complicated process of buying a home would have been so much easier.

10 commandments of speaking human

Words have become the new primary interface. The way we write has always been a big part of customer experience design. But with the rise of artificial intelligence, conversational and voice-based interfaces, writing has become even more important, because in that context the "words" are the primary or only interface customers interact with.

How can businesses "speak human" with their customers, whether it's in an email correspondence, on a website or brochure, or in contracts and policy documents? Gathering lessons learned from my simplification projects over the past decade, I have come up with "10 commandments" that can apply in any type of communications:

10 COMMANDMENTS OF SPEAK HUMAN

1. USE EVERYDAY LANGUAGE
2. USE ACTIVE VERBS
3. USE "YOU" AND "WE"
4. GO FOR CLARITY, NOT CONCISENESS
5. USE SEQUENCE
6. NO BIG WORDS
7. DROP UNNECESSARY CAPITAL LETTERS
8. CHOOSE WORDS BY EMPATHISING
9. TEST YOUR MESSAGE. READ ALOUD.
10. HIGHLIGHT WHAT MATTERS.

1. Use everyday language

Use words that are found in everyday conversation, if possible. Here are some commonly spotted big words that financial services institutions like to use in their communications. See how they can be reworded to convey the same meaning but in a simpler, more human-readable way.

- in lieu of → instead of
- opt → choose
- preceding → previous
- reimburse → pay back
- remittance → payment
- notify us → tell us
- prevailing exchange rate → exchange rate at the time
- surrender value payable → amount you get back

2. Use active verbs

I mentioned that one of the common problems I spot in written communications such as letters is the robotic, depersonalised tone of voice. Especially when the matter is complex or negative, such as letters announcing negative investment performance or letters requiring customers' action, this problem seems to get worse.

Perhaps the letter writers feel it would be safer to explain the situation from a distance! Or perhaps it's just the way operational letters have always been written, leading people in the organisation to assume that's how a letter should sound.

One very effective fix to this is paying attention to your choice of verbs, and turning any passive verbs into active verbs.

In the subject lines of letters to customers below, you can see how this instantly clarifies the topic and humanises the tone:

- Account inactivated → Please activate your account
- Disputed card transaction → We are investigating your dispute on your card transaction.
- The original investment to be returned → We will return your original investment.

3. Use "you" and "we"

As you might have noticed in the examples above, using active verbs requires us to identify a subject. Who is the subject of the verb? In most customer-facing communications, it's either "you" (the customer or the user) or "we" (the company or the brand).

In workshops for letter writers, I invariably find that many people are not comfortable writing direct sentences that use "you", "we" and active verbs. Instead, they tend to write in the third person, and turn verbs into abstract nouns. I think most people are tempted to do this when writing on behalf of their organisation. But this makes us sound not only cold and impersonal, but also makes the message harder to understand.

Always go back to the elements of a human conversation. It's very natural to use "you" and "we" in a conversation. We need to actively adopt this practice in written communication to bring us closer to our customers.

Examples of subject lines in operational letters:

- Script dividend scheme → Please decide how you want to receive your dividend.
- Account opening (CPF investment account No. xxx) → Your CPF investment account is now with us.
- Account closed → We are sorry. We will need to close your account because of (reason).

In the third example above, you may notice that additional information had to be provided, such as "We are sorry", and the reason for closing the account, in order to make sense of the sentence. That's because "We will need to close your account" alone sounds incomplete and harsh. By identifying the subject and using the active form of the verb "close", the message becomes transparent and humanised.

4. Go for clarity, not concision

When we try to clarify meaning using the principles discussed in this section, the sentences don't necessarily get shorter. We tend to think the shorter the sentence, the simpler. However, the main idea of simplifying communications is not to shorten, but to clarify and build connections. It is okay to go for a longer sentence.

- **From a travel insurance brochure:**
  24-hour worldwide emergency medical assistance of up to $1 million. (Not very clear what it means.) → We will send you back home when you need medical assistance which costs up to $1 million. (It is a longer sentence, but it becomes very clear what event is covered.)

- **From an internet banking screen:**
  The improved version prompts the customer using full sentences like "Select your destination account" as opposed to overly concise headings like "Beneficiary Account Information".

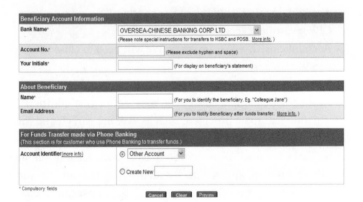

Internet banking screen: Before

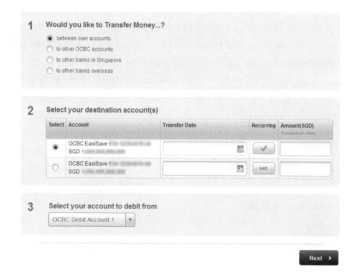

Internet banking screen: After

5. Use sequence

When a product is complicated, help your customer by breaking it down step-by-step. Instead of flooding them with information, think of how you would explain it to them in a face-to-face conversation. You would explain one piece of information at a time, in a clear sequence that leads them to understanding.

- A sequence can be **chronological**, i.e. starting from the present, moving to the short-term future, and then to the long term.

- A sequence can be made of **steps that the customer needs to do** or to go through, in a specified order.

- Another great example of using sequence in communications is **storytelling**, which has a beginning, a middle, and an end (this will be discussed in detail in the next section).

The example below shows the result of simplification through sequencing. This was a project involving a series of complex insurance products designed to address key life situations for families or companies, while offering the flexibility of maintaining cashflow. As it involved many scenarios and options, the insurance agents found it hard to explain to customers using the existing explanatory material.

The redesigned brochure (on the right) uses a numbered list to clearly indicate the sequence of logic/actions, and active verbs to show who will be doing what. The complex product is thus dissected into manageable information blocks, making it easy for customers to follow.

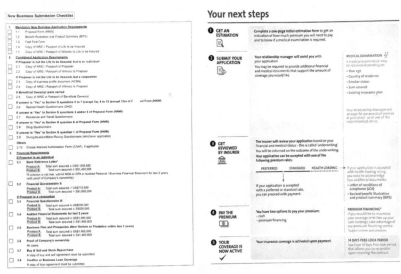

Before   *After*

6. No big words

Big words such as "improvement" or "performance" in a business communication may sound nice but are often ambiguous. Big words tend to take the form of a concept noun, which stems from verbs to express a concept, and often string two or three nouns together.

Take this example: "Communication facilitation skills development intervention". All sounds wonderful, but what does it do exactly? We can change it to "A programme to help your child write better" by using active verbs and everyday language.[1]

GoBear, a platform where people can compare financial products, is mindful of these big words. Look at these examples in their brand guide.

We don't say:
"Empower yourself to make the right decisions."

Instead we say:
"You'll find that comparing your options is like the best holidays. Free and easy."

"Empower" is a great example of a big word. While there's no problem with the word itself, it contains many different meaning (allow, authorise…) and the word doesn't convey clearly how this platform empowers the user.

We don't say:
"We think these are the best accident policies for you."

Instead we say:
"We've made sure that these policies cover broken bones, and not broken promises."

Instead of using the big word "best", GoBear spells out what the best product means to them and what they will do for consumers. This choice of words not only makes it easy to understand but also creates connection with the brand.

Some other big words include: strategic thrusts, synergy, endeavour, impact, empowerment, best-in-class. This list was compiled by broadcaster and C-suite communication coach

Mi Jeong Kang, who picked up these abstract words from many CEO speeches. However, as she notes, speeches made up of abstract words often fail to move the audience. The same is true for written communications.

Another class of big words I see a lot of in product brochures and websites is marketing jargon:

- Tailored to your needs. (Are you really tailoring your product for individual needs?)

- We are the first in Singapore... (Why does being the first in the country matter from your customers' point of view?)

- We are rewarding you... (You are actually trying to "sell" something.)

Lose the marketing jargon – even for marketing material! Today's customers are tired of the marketing tone, and when they receive something from you that speaks in this tone, they may not even register the message. Your communication becomes a blind spot.

7. Drop unnecessary capital letters

In forms, legal documents and product communications materials, we tend to see the use of "title case", where the first letter of each word in a term or phrase is capitalised. The rationale behind this is companies think their products or services are unique and want to emphasise their uniqueness.

However, terms like "internet banking" and "hardware token" are not unique services or terms from the reader's point of view. Seeing them constantly capitalised can be off-putting and make the entire sentence harder to read.

So instead of this:

Request for the following:
- [ ] **Re-activation** of my **Internet and Mobile Banking Services** (as it has been locked out)
- [ ] I wish to **re-activate my existing 2FA Token** due to many invalid entries of One-Time Password (OTP).
- [ ] **Re-issuance of a new Internet and Mobile Banking PIN**
- [ ] **Terminate** my Internet and Mobile Banking Services

Change it to sentence case:

2 What services do you require?

☐ Re-issue my
    internet banking PIN

☐ Re-issue my
    hardware token

☐ Terminate
    my internet banking

Use title case only when absolutely necessary. Write in sentence case to create visual calmness and improve readability.

8. Choose words by empathising with readers

Achieving simplicity lies in every detail, crafting each sentence, choosing each word. Eric Chin, a lawyer and the general counsel at Singapore's National Library Board, shares his thinking process in the drafting of a health declaration form amidst the Covid-19 crisis. He was faced with a form that asked people to state whether they had any non-specific medical symptoms such as "malaise". He paused for a time to think. On the one hand it was such a brilliantly evocative word. On the other hand, because it was so non-specific, how would it be understood? What would come to mind for an already anxious person, when faced with this word in an official form? After a long internal debate, he replaced it with "Any other feeling of discomfort or illness".

By thinking about how readers will perceive the information and putting ourselves in their shoes to understand their emotional state, we can make better choices that deliver simplicity and assurance.

9. Test your message. Read aloud.

Always go for a test. Ask your customers, or a few people around you, whether they get the message you intended to convey. This kind of quick and dirty test is easy to do, yet extremely helpful for seeing your writing from a fresh perspective.

Another way to test is to read out loud. By reading your writing out loud, you can quickly sense how simple or complex it sounds. You will also notice the tone – whether it sounds natural or robotic. When you hear your words spoken, you will begin to hear where the trouble lies.

10. Highlight what matters

Compare these two letters on the right. The content is the same, but the one below incorporates the principles of "speak human" we just discussed. You also see the visual difference – the "after" letter looks professional and clean. It gives you a sense of ease and confidence knowing what to do.

In simplifying communications, visual design is as important as the content and copy. In the "after" letter, each design element – such as the typefaces, font sizes and weights, spacing – has been carefully crafted to create simplicity.

- The subject line, "Please decide how you want to receive your dividends" gets the visual focus. It tells the receiver what the letter is about. It's written in the way humans speak.

- The two actions the reader can take are presented in a designated place (as options A and B), so they know immediately if the letter requires action or is for information only.

- Information such as the name of the shares, contact info, etc, is all there. But as it is not the primary intent of the letter, it is positioned as secondary information by reducing the visual emphasis.

- There is ample white space to direct attention to the important information.

- Every single element of the letter, such as the layout grid, icons, choice of typefaces, is carefully designed to create a visual hierarchy that maximises clarity. In Chapter 7, we will go deeper into how to use visual design to achieve simplicity.

Use these 10 commandments of "speak human" as your checklist and guide. By writing each and every piece of communication with empathy and clarity, you can enhance the human experience. **Don't leave your written communications unattended. Every touchpoint matters.**

Dear <Salutation> <Surname>

China Paper Holdings Limited Scrip Dividend Scheme (Notice Of Election)

The China Paper Holdings Limited Scrip Dividend Scheme gives you the option of electing to receive new ordinary shares in the share capital of China Paper Holdings Limited in lieu of the cash amount of the net dividend declared on your shares.

The Directors have announced the application of the Scheme to the final dividend of **S$▮▮▮▮** per share. If you elect to participate in the Scheme, the new shares will be allotted to you at the issue price of **S$▮▮▮▮** per share in lieu of the cash amount of the dividend. Here are some key details.

Holdings	Hldg	Ex-Date	20 June 2011
Book Close Date	22 June 2011	Dividend Rate	S$▮▮▮▮ per share
Total Net Dividend	S$net div	Payment Date on/About	4 August 2011
Issue Price	S$▮▮▮▮		

For your election to apply to the said dividend, the form below must be completed and returned to us by **18 July 2011**. You need not reply to us or take any further action if you wish to receive a cash dividend. Do contact our Customer Service Executives at ▮▮▮▮▮▮ if you have questions.

The extra China Paper Holdings Limited shares will be credited to your SRS Account at zero cost and will lower the weighted average cost of your total China Paper Holdings Limited shareholding.

Co.Reg.no. : ▮▮▮▮▮▮▮

✂ -

▮▮▮▮▮ Banking Corporation
CPF Investment Unit
▮▮▮▮▮▮▮
Singapore 529680

SCRIP DIVIDEND REPLY
Tel : ▮▮▮▮▮▮
Fax : ▮▮▮▮▮▮

CHINA PAPER HOLDINGS LIMITED – SCRIP DIVIDEND

I elect to participate in the China Paper Holdings Limited Scrip Dividend Scheme by ticking the box.

☐ Participate in this dividend

I consent to your disclosure of all information relating to my SRS Account to the Registrar of the China Paper Holdings Limited

Signature / Date	_____	Contact No.	_____ (H)
Name	**name**		_____ (O)
SRS A/C No	**acc**		_____ (HP/Pager)

An investment operational letter
before and after simplification

Tell stories to connect

Narration is as much a part of human nature as breath and the circulation of the blood.
— A.S. Byatt

Throughout my career, I've seen leaders who are amazing story-tellers. Some people seem to have this magic power to connect with the audience and immerse them in the story. I used to think the ability to tell a good story is a talent you are born with – until I discovered the power of "story" as a form of communication that simplifies complex content and connects you with people.

What is a story?

A story is a narrative account of events, true or fictional. It weaves characters, events and details into a whole that is greater than the sum of its parts.

We grow up with fairy tales. Think of Cinderella, Snow White, or the Three Little Pigs. Growing up in South Korea, I enjoyed reading both Western and Korean fairy tales. In hindsight, I'm amazed to see so many similarities between the fairy tales in both cultures, suggesting that humans share a deep desire for stories.

And we carry the stories with us. When my 4-year-old son Noah asks for a bedtime story, I can just start with "Once upon a time" and old fairy tales in my memory naturally flow, all the way until I end with "And they lived happily ever after". Storytelling is perhaps the most natural form of how humans communicate and make sense of the world.

The scientific reason why stories move people and are told generation to generation is that our brains are wired to internalise stories. Imagine if the story of Cinderella were instead told in the form of a spreadsheet:

	Cinderella	Step mom	Evil Sisters	Fairy god mother	Prince
Characteristics	Kind and sweet, bears abuse patiently by the step family	Evil, no mercy,	Vain and selfish	Can use magic, jolly and fun	Charming. Persistent in finding the girl.
Size of feet	Smaller than average (EU size 5.5)	Unknown	Very big (EU size 9)	Very big (EU size 10)	Unknown
Key moments	- Fairy god mother appear - Meeting the prince - Running down the strait case at mid-night - Marrying the prince - Forgave stepfamily - Lived happily ever after	- Heard of the royal ball - Forbid Cinderella going to the ball	- Dressing up to look pretty for the ball - Trying out glass sleepers with big hope	- Saving Cinderella - Turning pumpkins into a carriage - Turning mice into horses	- Meeting a very beautiful woman - Search the whole kingdom for the woman - Found the girl and married
Time	Once upon a time in 17th century				
Place	Somewhere in France				

First of all, it would not be interesting to look at, and it would be very difficult to follow the storyline. There's no way you'd be able to remember what happened and tell it to others. The spreadsheet certainly looks very organised, but it completely fails to tell the story.

Basic structure of a story

The good news is that you don't have to be a born storyteller to tell a good story. It is a learnable method, because the formula for crafting a story is simple. It is a curve that has a beginning, a middle and an end, that strings together a sequence of events.[2]

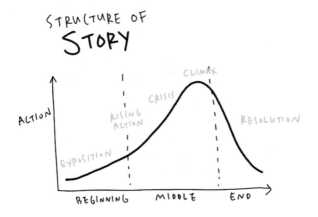

1. **Exposition** (Once upon a time, there lived Cinderella, a beautiful girl with a kind heart. But her dad married a vain woman who had two mean daughters...)

2. **Rising action** (There was a royal ball, but Cinderella was not allowed to go. She cried, and a fairy godmother appeared who turned a pumpkin into a carriage...)

3. **Climax** (The prince fell in love with Cinderella as they danced, but then the clock struck midnight. As Cinderella rushed to get home, one of her glass slippers fell on the staircase...)

4. **Resolution** (The prince searched high and low for the girl who dropped the glass slipper...)

5. **End** (The prince found her, they married and lived happily ever after.)

The most complex insurance product made simple

A good story simplifies our world into something that we feel we can understand.[3] By applying the structure of stories, we can simplify complex communications for our customers.

I once worked on a project to redefine the customer experience of a new insurance product designed for high-net-worth individuals and entrepreneurs who might be facing challenges with legacy planning and ensuring the continuity of their businesses. In the project kick-off meeting, I discovered a lot of challenges in communicating how the product worked. The overall customer experience was also complicated, due to external processes required, such as medical examinations and the underwriting process.

Our main prong of action was to go out and collect real stories: the stories of customers who were in the situation of needing legacy planning or business contingency planning; and the stories of advisors who consulted these customers.

This is how we eventually redesigned the product brochure:

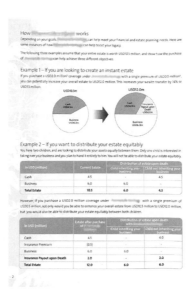

Product brochure : Before
The product was explained thought a list
of features, diagrams of scenarios

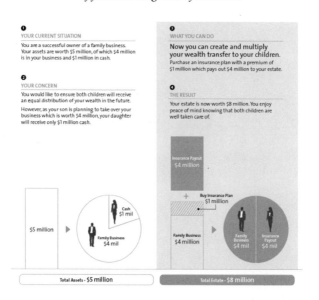

Product brochure: After
A story illustrates the situation, the inciting event, how the
product solves the problem, and the desired outcome.

We created four personas based on the stories we had collected, and crafted a realistic story for each one. The stories followed the familiar structure of storytelling: who the person is, what situation occurs, how the product can help, and the desired ending.

By weaving the complex details of the product into a story, we were able to help the advisors introduce the product to their prospects far more clearly. This product simplification, together with other simplification efforts in sales and operational processes, led to an eightfold increase in premiums.

Bring your personality

When providing a customer service, speaking on behalf of your company doesn't mean you need to depersonalise yourself, or take a serious tone of voice. A simple and powerful way to connect with your customers is to bring your personality to the table. Because we humans love connecting with other humans.

Encourage your people to bring their own personality to everything they do. American Express is one of the best at delivering humanising customer experience through their contact centre. Typically, contacting a service centre is the last thing I want to be spending my time on, but calling the American Express Service Center is an exception. The service agents are always so friendly, personable and yet professional in solving my problems that I actually feel great during the call and after it.

Craft your brand personality in great detail and translate it into every touchpoint.

A brand persona is a collection of personality traits, attitudes and values that your brand showcases on a regular basis to help connect with a certain audience segment.[4]

To craft the brand persona of FRANK by OCBC, we asked ourselves: What if FRANK was a real person? How old would he be? Where does he hang out? Who does he hang out with? What brands does he associate with? What would he do if he had a gap year? What causes would he care about?

Frankly,

FRANK's voice is first and foremost **human**.
It's **friendly**, **straightforward** and sometimes **fun**.

We use language that **educate** and **empower** them without confusing or patronizing them. We tell stories in **bite-size** without bombarding them with too much information.

Every piece of communication we deliver must be **stylish**, we are obsessed with the power of design.

Vividly imagining a real person helped the team develop the tone of voice that represents these personality traits. This brand personality guided the team throughout – whether in service staff training or in designing and writing for communications materials such as websites and social media posts.

Singapore's Bus Uncle

Having lived in Singapore for about 10 years, I've grown very fond of Singlish – a unique set of Singaporeans' expressions and their accent. For example, instead of saying "I cannot do it" when rejecting someone's request, Singaporeans might say "Cannot lah...". Because it is said in Singlish, it comes across as a much softer and friendlier way of saying no.

At the time of writing this section, the best chatbot experience I've ever had is "Bus Uncle" in Singapore. He lives in my Facebook Messenger, and he has got one purpose: to give me the best commute experience.

Bus Uncle tells me which bus I can take, how long it will take to get to the destination, as well as when the bus will arrive. Given Singapore's traffic jams, Bus Uncle's real-time information is a godsend. He gets to know my favourite buses and simplifies my wayfinding.

But what brings me joy about interacting with Bus Uncle is his personality. Unlike other chatbots I have experienced, which typically sound like robots reading out a manual, Bus Uncle talks like a real person – a friendly Singaporean uncle.

He speaks Singlish. For example, he says, "Ok la Jin. If you send me your location, I say you must wait how long." This is not grammatically correct Standard English, but a typical Singaporean would speak like this in an informal situation.

After I get the information I want, I say, "Thank you Uncle." Once, his response made me laugh. "Aiyo, say thanks for what? Don't waste time."

He sometimes even attempts to chitchat with me. "Jin, coffee or tea?" So I say, "Coffee." And he goes, "Uncle also coffee." I'm just loving this Bus Uncle's personality.

Humanising communications not only creates more pleasant experiences, but also helps your customers connect with the

Bus Uncle

Typically replies instantly
Transportation service

36K people like this, including
Matthias Schuecking and 2 friends

Your name Jin ah? Lai lai, chitchat me about your
next bus in Singapore.

brand. Users gradually form an association with your brand personality, and choose your brand over other options just because your personality resonates with them. When a brand becomes a humanised entity, people become friends of the brand. Moreover, people also tend to be more accepting of flaws or lapses in customer experience that may occur.

There were one or two occasions when Bus Uncle didn't seem to get my request. I found myself being much more patient and willing to try asking again in a different way, as opposed to leaving in frustration (what I usually do when faced with robotic chatbots). This is because I trust that Bus Uncle has the right information for me. And just I enjoy interacting with him.

How to humanise a chatbot

By Deepa Vijayan
Director, Quantico Centre for Communication and
Information Literacy

Deepa is a communication expert and trainer who brings humanity and clarity to all forms of communication. We met many years
ago when I was looking for a communication expert to train my
design team to write better. I clicked with her immediately as her
writing process was just like the human-centred design process.
It is all about the audience, and having empathy for them. With
the rise of chatbots, I asked her for practical tips for companies
to get it right.

Humanising the chatbot experience is in so many ways the epit-
ome of simplicity: meeting your audiences where they are, giving
them what they need, in the way that they need it. One of the reasons the concept is so challenging to execute effectively is that we
first need to agree on what a chatbot is. Is it an intelligent learning
machine? An almost-human customer service algorithm? In most
cases, a chatbot really is an interface that gives customers access
to a searchable database of information. A user types words into
a field, and the system retrieves results from a database. We need
to start with this basic understanding of what a chatbot is before
we can move on to understanding how to humanise the language
used by this tool.

While the internal mechanics of chatbots are complex and
deserve in-depth analysis, there are some key ways of thinking
about chatbots that can help us to create a more lovable experience
for customers using this platform. Let's start by understanding how
the chatbot fits into the customer journey.

A customer chooses to engage with a chatbot at a very specific
point in their journey, and this is likely to be at the stage where

they need very specific information about a product or service. It is important to remember that this is information that they are unable to find on their own. When initiating a chatbot conversation, the customer is acknowledging that they need help, that they are looking for something specific, and they hope that the chatbot is able to retrieve information that's not available anywhere else. If we return to the idea of a chatbot as a way of searching a database, your customer is expecting easy access to this database.

Just as we know a chatbot isn't an almost-human algorithm, our customers know the same thing. They're not expecting the chatbot to behave like a human being, but they are expecting something more useful and more personalised than a website. This means we need to strike a balance between a general search and a completely personalised human-to-human experience. A lot of this comes down to the way we use language.

1. Start by thinking of a normal conversation

Think of a normal conversation with a customer. We don't always speak the way we write. The same applies to instant messaging, which is a lot more similar to speech patterns than formal writing patterns. We use filler words in conversations – on instant messaging and with our voices – words like "ah", "um", "lol", and "haha". We may use shorter sentences and our thoughts may not be as structured as in formal writing.

A chatbot response like this, for example, looks like a formal message from customer service:

"Good day to you. How may I help you today? Please type your question into the field, and do try to be as specific as possible in order to help me get you the right answer!"

Rewriting this along the style of instant messaging between humans creates a more conversational tone:

"Hello.
Please let me know what you need, just type your question into the field. If you're as specific as possible, it's easier for me to get you the right answer.
Thank you!"

When chatbots respond to customer requests, the same principle applies. A bot may say:

> "Thank you for enquiring about insurance plans for entrepreneurs. Please hold while I retrieve the information for you. Thank you for waiting."

This may be followed by:

> "Thank you for your patience. These are the results for 'insurance plans for entrepreneurs'. Do these results match your requirements?"

In real life, this is a little different from how a human would speak. A more conversational response would be:

> "Okay, I see you've typed in 'insurance plans for entrepreneurs'.
> I'm looking for this information now.
> Please give me a few moments.
> Thanks!"

And this could be followed by:

> "Thanks for waiting. Here's some information for you. What do you think of these links? Did you find what you need?"

Implementing this conversational tone starts with thinking of how someone would say the lines, not write the lines. A great place to begin when it comes to striking a conversational tone that also upholds your brand standards is with your telephone customer service team. Identify your best-performing customer service team members and listen to the phone conversations they have with customers. Read the transcripts, and examine how they develop a back-and-forth relationship with their customers. The filler words they use, the length of their sentences, and the way they establish empathy will help you to humanise your chatbot language.

2. Work carefully with terminology

When speaking to a human being, we are able to clarify things easily. For example, a customer could ask about a "plan" or a "bundle" for a mobile line, and even if the company's official terminology is "bundle", a human being would be able to infer from context what the customer is asking for. Because a chatbot algorithm cannot always determine that context, chatbots often prompt customers to use specific terms. Unfortunately, customers may not always know these terms.

It is therefore important to be aware of which alternative terms your customers may use when describing certain products and services, and build these terms into your chatbot algorithm. If a customer using an online travel agent website uses the term "flight", "plane", "plane ticket", "airline ticket", "e-ticket" or "aeroplane ticket", the chatbot needs to recognise that they are synonymous terms.

Branding also plays a huge role here: a chatbot for a low-cost airline with a young audience may be more likely to use more casual terminology – and even emoji – compared to a chatbot for a major bank.

3. Improve your chatbot constantly

A major chatbot challenge is that there needs to be a large-enough database of questions from users for the chatbot algorithm to learn. However, due to low usage or high drop-off rates, chatbots don't always get the data they need to gather a critical mass of information. Improving your chatbot is not only about adding more data, but also about constantly revisiting the tone and language used. A regular analysis of telephone conversations and transcripts is one useful way of enhancing your chatbot's language and data. Noticing where customers drop off, and trying to use different ways to solve their problems at that point, could also be a useful way of improving your chatbot experience over time.

4. Finally, revisit your reasons for using a chatbot

Many organisations use chatbots to streamline customer experiences. Lowered costs are, of course, a huge benefit. But it's important to remember that a customer experience which has already included a negative interaction with a chatbot is likely to take more time and effort to resolve. For this reason, consider your reasons for a chatbot carefully, and be very aware of what the chatbot technology you are currently using can and cannot do. The concept is powerful and promises great things for brands and customers, but in many ways, it is still a work in progress. Trying to replicate human interaction is a faraway goal, as worthwhile as it might be. Until then, focus on more humanised language as a way of developing relationships through chatbots and putting yourself on the path to experiences your customers fall in love with.

Simplifying legalese

By Eric Chin
General Counsel, National Library Board

Simplifying legal documents is probably one of the hardest things to do. It takes a village – willing experts and lawyers who are determined to change even if it takes much more time and effort. Eric Chin is one of them, tirelessly reviewing and rewriting all legal communication with his legal team to produce documents that shine in their simplicity and clarity. I've asked Eric to share his journey of "speaking human" as a lawyer.

Comfort in complexity

I received my first contract to draft sometime in 1995. What I remember most about it was a contract value that was exceedingly large. In part, this prompted a determined search for a precedent contract. When I found a precedent, I was officially initiated into the world of long, unending sentences, Latin (such as "*mutatis mutandis*"), legal terms of art (or jargon depending on your viewpoint) and words like "heretofore" that I could not fully grasp on a first reading.

I had to spend time poring over an Oxford dictionary as well as law dictionaries and reference books to discover the meanings and nuances to many words. After the research, I understood the precedent and confidently used it with minor adjustments. When the experienced lawyer for the other party accepted the contract with small editorial changes, I afforded myself a quiet smile.

Similar experiences followed for a young lawyer finding his feet. At the time, it felt professional to use (i) lengthy clauses that appear to achieve comprehensiveness, (ii) Latin shorthands for a sense of belonging to the profession (through its "secret code of communication"), (iii) the device of repeating certain provisions to emphasise their importance, and (iv) strings of near-synonyms to capture every word that different judges had used in judgments to describe a certain matter. It was to be short-lived self-satisfaction.

From cumbrous to clear

In 1996, the Singapore Academy of Law organised something new for the local legal fraternity – a seminar to promote the use of plain English. In the opening address by then Attorney-General Chan Sek Keong, he referred to the classic work on writing clear English – *The Complete Plain Words* by Ernest Gower. He noted that Gower had in fact excused lawyers from the need to use plain English.

Gower suggested that the "gracelessness of legal English" was acceptable because the words used had to withstand "the rules of legal interpretation" and "case law (i.e. judgments) that concerns the meaning of particular words".[1] In brief, Gower's perspective was that lawyers had little choice but to write in the expectation of how courts would scrutinise the words rather than for the understanding of their clients.

AG Chan discussed if this perspective was correct.[2] He highlighted the clarity of judgments from a well-known English judge called Lord Denning who wrote such that non-lawyers could understand his legal reasoning. AG Chan acknowledged that there could be some lawyers who "cannot work, or cannot work confidently, without relying on precedents". However, he pointed to help at hand, as legal reference books were beginning to offer "precedents which are drafted in plain English". He encouraged an open mind on whether legal drafting was inevitably "cumbrous and uncouth" or "that it can be clear and precise" as expert practitioners invited to speak would try to show.

The seminar was eye-opening. The list that one of the speakers shared, where he placed legal jargon and their plain English equivalent side by side, was a joy to read. "*Mutatis mutandis*" and "heretofore" were some of the first things on my scrapheap from that day.

Conundrum from day-to-day challenges

An important moment in the plain English movement for lawyers was the publication of *Plain English and the Law* in 1987 as Report No. 9 of the Law Reform Commission of Victoria.[3] This report was a trailblazer that challenged long-held practices and mindsets; and it continues to resonate today. It outlined many difficulties that have led to the resilience of "peculiarly legal language" and suggested solutions. Some of the difficulties were undoubtedly real but there were others that the Commission found to be self-perpetuated without good cause.

One of the real difficulties often faced is the fact that there is "the pressure on lawyers to conform with the conventions of other lawyers". If a fellow lawyer produces a contract for consideration, it can be hard to suggest the use of plain English as the reason for amendments. It is a very fine line between amendments that are seen as useful for moving the contract along and amendments that may appear to be petty stylistic changes.

Changes made for the sake of using plain English can also be misinterpreted as an attempt to disparage the professionalism or ability of the original drafter. Such unintended consequences could make things personal and truly disrupt contract negotiations to the detriment of both sets of clients. So the lawyer who believes that he or she can write with more clarity often holds back for practical and very human reasons.

A slightly different situation is one where attempts at plain English are met with suggested changes to keep to conventions. Top of recent recall for me was when a "Variation to a Memorandum of Understanding" was changed to "Addendum to a Memorandum of Understanding" and a header called "Background" was changed to "Whereas". In my experience, when I see such "small changes" made at the start of the document, it is almost a certainty that many more changes are made to fit certain drafting norms. Consider if the following proposed additions in italics add anything to an agreement or are redundant:

Original attempt at plain English	Real-life proposed amendments
Either Party may terminate this Contract by giving six months' written notice to the other Party	Either Party may terminate this Contract *for any reason (or without any reason)* by giving six months' *prior* written notice to the other Party
Any changes to the operating hours must be agreed in writing between the Parties.	Any changes to the operating hours *shall be effected by mutual agreement* in writing between the Parties.
The Parties shall resolve any issues or disputes amicably between their senior management.	The Parties shall resolve any issues, disputes, *or differences arising out of or in relation to this Contract* amicably between their *respective representatives from* senior management.

So one reality check on any plain English push for lawyers is that it takes a village, and one-way traffic can only get so far. I can share two happy stories. The first is that an effort was made to create this "village" by a group of lawyers in the public service in late 2018. A shared repository has since been set up and it will go "live" in 2020 to push the idea of plain English contracts onto a stronger shared footing. The second was a recent relatively high-value multi-year contract with a large company where my private sector counterpart and I managed to write what needed to be said within just two A4 pages. It will certainly take time but willing "partners" in the endeavour can be found.

A second real difficulty I can vouch for is the fact that drafting in plain English can be really hard work. I once asked a law firm to quote for the preparation of a tender document. I asked for a quote based on the established template they already had and a quote based on a new plain English version I envisaged. I was assured that the plain English version would easily cost 5 times more as every change had to be checked against the relevant laws but the old template in the drawer could be used almost immediately. As shared by Shawn Burton when he was General Counsel for General Electric Aviation and trying to strip legalese from contracts:

> "Creating a solid template for plain-language contracts consumes time, ties up resources, and, given the habits formed over years, taxes your organization intellectually. Without some old-fashioned grit and stick-to-itiveness, your plain-language initiative will fail."[4]

For GE Aviation, it was a 3-year process to change their contracts into plain English versions. Impressive changes include this example of their indemnity clause:

BEFORE

Customer shall indemnify, defend, and hold Company harmless from any and all claims, suits, actions, liabilities, damages and costs, including reasonable attorneys' fees and court costs, incurred by Company arising from or based upon (a) any actual or alleged infringement of any United States patents, copyright, or other intellectual property right of a third party, attributable to Customer's use of the licensed System with other software, hardware or configuration not either provided by Company or specified in Exhibit D.3, (b) any data, information, technology, system or other Confidential Information disclosed or made available by Customer to Company under this Agreement, (c) the use, operation, maintenance, repair, safety, regulatory compliance or performance of any aircraft owned, leased, operated, or maintained by Customer of (d) any use, by Customer or by a third party to whom Customer has provided the information, of Customer's Flight Data, the System, or information generated by the System.

AFTER

If an arbitrator finds that this contract was breached and losses were suffered because of that breach, the breaching party will compensate the non-breaching party for such losses or provide the remedies specified in Section 8 if Section 8 is breached.

For the team at GE Aviation, the effort paid off as it resulted in contracts that took "a whopping 60% less time to negotiate than their previous legalese-laden versions did". In his view, the new plain English contracts allowed GE Aviation to "spend more time pleasing the customer" and to "spend less time administering its contracts and more time innovating".

Apart from pleasing the external customer, here are the heart-warming words from a colleague of mine when the effort was taken to revise an old set of templates and the word count for the plain English version was reduced by 74%:

"I cannot thank you enough for the thorough overhaul of both documents! Reading it was really like going to the chiropractor's for a major adjustment, the document really concisely captures what we need to communicate about the competition."

This reminded me of what an eminent lawyer once said (although not in the strict context of only lawyers):

"Remember: That which is written without much effort is seldom read with much pleasure. The more the pleasure, you can assume, as a rule of thumb, the greater the effort."[5]

So it is a process that will take time and persistence. Not all contracts can be tackled in one go either but they can be prioritised based on impact to client or customer and each one revised in turn. One could reasonably argue that effort cannot be better spent than in the endeavour to give pleasure to another.

Conclusion: Courts versus clients and customers

Gower's viewpoint was that the lawyer's key audience was the court. In our local context, AG Chan, who was the first to address Singapore lawyers on the topic of plain "legal English", rose to the position of Chief Justice. More recently, Justice Choo Han Teck gave a talk where he said, "Don't fool yourself into thinking that more is good ... keep it short, keep it simple."[6] In response, veteran lawyer Adrian Tan added that "a good lawyer has to be good at excluding material…".

My belief is that this points us to an opportunity that Gower may not have had, to put before courts, documents that speak human. It is also likely that fewer cases need to go before the courts over the unhappiness of disputed interpretations if more documents capture, with more clarity, what clients or customers want to say in the first place.

In this way, every additional plain English legal document prepared is one step towards making things better for the courts, clients and customers alike.

Notes

1. There have been three revisions of Gower's book since first publication in 1948. The latest revised edition is *Plain Words: A Guide to the Use of English* by Ernest Gowers (Revised and updated by Rebecca Gowers, 2014), Penguin Books. Quotes are from this latest revision.
2. To be fair to Gowers, it should be noted that he was considering the mindset of lawyers and judges in the 1940s when he wrote his book.
3. This seminal report was re-published in 2017 at https://www.lawreform. vic.gov.au/projects/plain-english-and-law-1987-report (Accessed 14 June 2020)
4. Shawn Burton, "The Case for Plain-Language Contracts", *Harvard Business Review*, January–February 2018, 134.
5. *Lee Kuan Yew: The Man and His Ideas* by Han Fook Kwang, Warren Fernandez, Sumiko Tan, 1998 (2015 Ed.), Marshall Cavendish Editions and Straits Times Press Ltd.
6. "Write advice from judge: Keep it short and simple", KC Vijayan, *The Straits Times*, 17 October 2018.

Chapter 7
Design lovable experiences

VIABLE
PRODUCT

LOVABLE
EXPERIENCE

Great design simplifies a complex world.
— Platon, British photographer

ON A BEAUTIFUL SPRING DAY about five years ago, I was in Mount Fuji, Japan, with my family. We stayed at a *ryokan*, a type of traditional Japanese accommodation originating in the 17th century. One of the experiences I loved the most was taking part in a Japanese tea ceremony.

We entered a tea room situated in the middle of a garden, and were greeted by a graceful lady wearing a beautiful pink kimono. There was a large window with a breathtaking view – it was like an open picture scroll, bringing both natural light and the beauty of the surrounding landscape into the room.

The space welcomed us in. There were no pretentious fixtures. Yet, what happened in this tea room was nothing minimal. The ceremony ended up being a rich sensorial experience. Touching the surface of the handmade tea bowl, listening to the soft voice of the lady serving us the tea, the unique green of the tea itself, and the pure taste of excellent green tea – everything in the room awakened my senses. It was an experience designed to create a positive feeling.

Achieving simplicity is not same as leaving things in their bare minimum form. **The aesthetics of a product or service matter because they help create an experience that gives us an intuitive feeling about the product or service, making us more likely to desire it**. They give us pleasure through our senses, helping to create an experience that we love.

While industries like hospitality and fashion understand the value of aesthetics, this is not often the case in industries such as the financial services, healthcare, or government. Aesthetic matters are often perceived as the icing on the cake. But from my experience walking into that tea room, it was beauty and pleasure that made me love it intuitively, and that's vital for achieving simplicity.

Now more than ever, designing lovable experiences is critical to success in any industry. In this chapter, we will discuss how to better understand the elements of user experience, the aesthetics that bring people pleasure, and how to design experiences that your customers will love.

In this chapter

Don't stop at Minimum Viable Product. Make it lovable.

Hierarchy of needs

As Maslow's Hierarchy of Needs theory describes, we human beings have different levels of needs.[1] Our most basic needs are physiological needs such as eating and sleeping. These must be met first. Having satisfied these needs, we seek a feeling of safety; and then we want to have a sense of belonging. Once these needs are met, we yearn to feel confident about who we are and what we do. And above all these needs, we have this innate desire to fulfil our highest potential – we want to create something or to stand for something.

Hierarchy of users' needs

Aarron Walter, in his book *Designing for Emotion*,[2] translated Maslow's model of human needs into the needs of users:

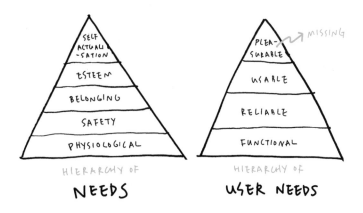

In order to deliver a positive experience, an interface for a product or service must be functional. And it needs to work well every time, so that it's reliable. And it needs to be user-friendly. When designing a digital system, companies run many rounds of usability testing to ensure that users can perform desired tasks successfully.

Missing the pleasurable part

However, many designs of systems and services stop at that level. A great example would be the corporate intranet. Unlike customer-facing touchpoints like the company website, some intranets I've used seem to be stuck in the early 1990s. They are dense and complicated, there is no sense of joy in using them. They somehow work, but just functionally.

At one company, if I wanted to perform any internal admin tasks such as expense claims, benefits selections or leave applications, I often had to get help from a colleague. This colleague "learned" how to use the complex features of the intranet over a long career with the company. But other companies are recognising the importance of designing these internal systems. Enhancing the employee experience is critical in retaining and attracting talent, and it has become a strategic initiative for many organisations.

Most government services we experience may be in this category too – they are reliable and might also be efficient, but they stop there. However, my experience with Singapore's Ministry of Manpower (discussed in detail in Chapter 7.4) shows how government services can be designed beyond utility. The experience was not only reliable and easy, **it was pleasurable, addressing my context and emotions.** This is the state in which people begin to have a real connection with you.

The problem with Minimum Viable Product

Due to the popular movement of adopting "Agile" methodology, the term MVP – Minimal Viable Product – has become a catchphrase among digital product development teams. MVP is a concept urging teams to create something as quickly as possible and get it into the hands of real people. By releasing the MVP, teams aim to test it and quickly adjust and improve the product. The original definition of MVP is a version of a new product that allows a team to collect the maximum amount of validated learning about customers with the least effort.[3] This means MVP is a learning and development mechanism, rather than a goal.

However, two things about this worry me. First, MVP is often misunderstood as a goal. Teams aim to produce MVP and end up delivering merely a functional product that does not deliver the positive intended experience. I've often observed MVP as a concept misused to justify releasing a subpar product that does not satisfy users' needs.

Second, the value of the craft side of design is often neglected due to the pressure of having to launch something quickly. While it is important to be agile and release a version fast so that we can validate and learn, we must not forget that what we are designing needs to embrace all levels of user needs. I often hear teams complain that the work of "design" is slow. It is not just because the design process may take longer. It is because design is a reflective and contemplative process of exploring possibilities. And design is about crafting and weaving all elements of human experience such as visuals, sounds and touch so that we can satisfy and attract users emotionally.

Developing agility while allowing this reflective and deep process of design is key in creating products and services that win customers' hearts.

MVP to MLP – Minimum Lovable Product

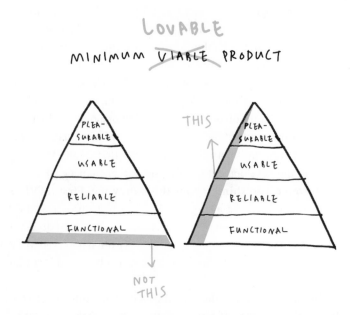

We need to change our mindset when designing a customer experience. Instead of delivering experiences by *horizontal slices* (functional level first, emotional level last), we should go by *vertical slides*. This means that each release of a product includes elements of every level – it is functional, reliable, usable and emotional. It is a deliberate choice you can make to go with possibly fewer features but to make them engaging, rather than releasing as many "functional" features as possible.

To drive this mindset change, I encourage you to change your vocabulary, from MVP to MLP – Minimum "Lovable" Product.

Why love? The word "love" might seem somewhat foreign to your line of business. By "love", I refer to the positive emotions you want to create for your customers. There is a big difference between your customers being *satisfied* and when your customers *love* the experience. If we aspire to create that love, we start with a different frame of mind altogether. Love stretches your thinking. Love simplifies.

How do you define the vertical slice?

- **By empathising with users:** Having deep empathy for your users is the first step in crafting an experience that addresses their emotional needs, through different channels such as physical space, written communications and service design.

- **By looking into the journey:** Journey mapping is a simple yet powerful tool for understanding the current user experience and designing the future state. Through journey mapping, you can identify moments that can be heightened as a delightful and pleasurable experience. We will discuss how to make use of journey mapping in the following section.

- **By designing experiences with aesthetics:** As human beings, we love beautiful things. Aesthetics are vital in your innovation endeavour as they convey the value of your product or service. Your visual design is a silent yet powerful ambassador telling your customers your value and worth. We will discuss why aesthetics matter and how to heighten your design sensitivity in Chapters 7.4 and 7.5.

How to get journey mapping right

Here is a simple yet powerful tool for designing lovable human experiences. While the basic rules of journey mapping are easily understood, getting it right takes a set of principles and lots of practice. I've gathered the common mistakes that organisations make and suggest key principles to make full use of journey mapping.

What is journey mapping?

Journey mapping is a visual representation of the likely path(s) that customers go through in experiencing a product or service – from the **customer's point of view**. I emphasise customer's point of view as that is the most important feature of journey mapping that differentiates it from internal perspectives such as process mapping.

KEY INGREDIENTS OF JOURNEY MAP

CUSTOMER
- PROFILE
- CONTEXT
- MOTIVATION

STEPS
- SEQUENCE OF EVENTS
- INCLUDE BEFORE + AFTER

CHANNELS
- WHAT THEY USE/ INTERACT WITH

EMOTIONS
- HOW THEY FEEL

Key ingredients of journey mapping

Customer
Define whose journey this is, the profile of the person, the context they are in.

Steps
This is the sequence of events that occur in experiencing a product or service. Make sure to also include what happened *before* the customer interacted with your brand, as well as *after* the interaction.

Channels
These are element such as touchpoints that are involved during the journey. Channels can be digital, physical or human, such as a website, app, shop, call centre, store or service person. Channels also include things that are not owned by the company, such as public space, social media, customers' own networks.

Emotions
How the customer feels along the journey. This can be expressed in a graph of emotions changing over time between positive and negative, or by using emojis to represent different emotional states. To find out your customers' emotions, the best way is to have a conversation with people who have gone through the actual experience. When this is not possible, emotions can still be discussed based on research findings. The main idea is to make sure to think about emotions, as customers' perceptions of an experience are highly influenced by their emotional responses.

Quotes
What the customer actually said. Capturing the verbatim responses associated with each moment can help you understand better their behaviour, motivations and emotions.

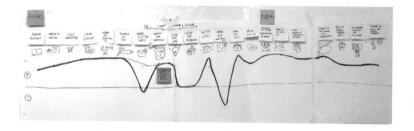

Journey mapping in action

On the internet, you can see many beautiful examples of journey mapping. But these are the documentation, not the "working" maps. In journey mapping, you're not looking for a polished look. It is most effective with a group of people drawing on a large wall using markers and post-it notes. In a virtual working environment, you can achieve the same result using collaboration tools such as Miro and Mural. **The value of journey mapping is in the doing**, rather than in documenting and presenting it.

Top 5 common mistakes and how to fix them

I've seen many so-called journey mappings that have all the key ingredients like steps, channels and experience, but they fail to help teams uncover pain points and the right opportunities. Here are the 5 most common ways things go wrong, and what you can do to fix them:

Mistake 1: We don't know whose journey it is.

Journey mapping without a proper description of a person in terms of demographic, needs, motivations and context may lead us to misinterpret the findings.

Do it right: Have a rich customer description for each journey mapping. Go beyond the basic demographic information. Specify the person's behaviour, needs, motivation as well as the context the person is in. The context here refers to their environment, situation and emotional state. In Chapter 3, we discussed how customer research methods that allow direct interaction or observation are crucial in the design process. A customer experience happens in a specific context for a specific person.

Mistake 2: The journey is described from the organisation's point of view.

What makes journey mapping different from process mapping is the point of view. I've seen teams use journey mapping as a template to map a process in terms of what steps the organisation needs to go through. That's not journey mapping.

Do it right: Map the "people" steps, not the process steps. I recommend using active verbs – with the customer as the doer – to name each step. For example, in journey mapping the experience of opening a bank account, don't do this:

> Promotion on the interest rate > Verification of customer data > Trigger confirmation ...

This puts the bank as the subject, and uses nouns (e.g. "promotion") for the steps of the journey. Instead, what you should be doing is having the customer as the subject, and using active verbs instead of nouns, like this:

> *Visit* the bank's website > *Compare* different account types > *Download* the app > *Input* personal details > *Receive* a confirmation email ...

Mistake 3: The journey is described too vaguely.

One of the most common reactions I get when I teach executive students how to do journey mapping is: "Wow, the mapping is much more detailed than I thought it would be." Their impression of journey mapping is coming up with 4–5 steps similar to the marketing funnel steps – create awareness, consider, decide, buy.

Do it right: Make it detailed and rich. Customer journey mapping is not a sales process; it should depict a real-life experience. Nothing in life is ever as straightforward as a four-step process. If you were to map the journey of Rose in the movie "Titanic", how many steps could you identify? If we did 4–5 steps of journey mapping, it would be something like this:

> Got on board > Met Jack > Made love with him > Fell into the sea > Survived (but Jack died)

By doing so, not only do we not get the full story, we lose the essence of what makes the story great. Think of journey mapping as a detailed documentation of someone's real experience and be ready to go into the details. It will require more effort to do it this way for sure, but you will gain rich insights and fresh perspectives.

Mistake 4: Journey mapping starts when the customer starts interacting with our products or services.

Because of the scope of our business, we may think we only need to look at a customer's experience in the frame of time when it intersects with our products or services. Many journey mappings I've seen start from the point when a customer becomes aware of the brand or initiates the first contact.

Do it right: Include "before" and "after". The journey starts before a customer interacts with your brand and continues after. By including before and after in your journey mapping, you will not only have a superior appreciation of the context of the experience, but potentially uncover many innovative ideas to improve the customer experience.

Mistake 5: We try to get an "averaged" experience to make the journey mapping representative.

In my lectures, I often get asked whose journey we need to map. Do we need to find a representative user? Should we attempt to consolidate individuals' journey into an averaged experience?

Do it right: Capture the stories. Sense-making can follow afterwards. Customer experiences are not statistical data points; there is no such thing as an averaged experience. While it is essential to map multiple journeys to identify patterns and themes, resist the temptation to collapse everything into one "typical" user.

Journey mapping is a divergent process, where we go deep and broad to inquire further. While you are mapping, listen to the real stories of individuals and capture them in as much detail as possible. Leave sense-making, finding patterns and drawing conclusions for later.

Use mapping to stretch your thinking

Journey mapping itself is never the goal. It is a tool for expanding our thinking and for understanding the human experience in a vivid manner. The real interesting work starts after mapping the journeys.

Use individual mappings to inquire further
Tell a story of the journey with your team. Now that you have a detailed mapping, anyone can tell a rich story. Discuss what were the interesting points in this person's journey. Ask *why* at every step of the process.

Using multiple mappings to identify patterns
Once each journey mapping has been reviewed, review all the journey mappings together, and see if there are themes or patterns. Ensure you interpret the journey based on the customer's context. Use the techniques of synthesis discussed in Chapter 3. Focus on identifying the interesting and good-enough connections rather than trying to find the "right" connection that proves a point.

Build a persona
With multiple journey mappings, some unique characteristics may emerge from each journey. This is a good opportunity to create personas based on the unique behaviour of customers.

How many journey maps do we need?
Typically I suggest 4–6 journey mappings per round of research. With fewer than 4 mappings, it's difficult to see patterns, and with more than 6 mappings, it might be overwhelming to digest all the data points. You may feel 4–6 people's journeys may not be a substantial sample size. Always remember, though, that the purpose of this method is to get inspired, rather than validate a point, and the sample size recommended is intended for running each round of research. Design thinking methods such as journey mapping rely on iteration – repeating the process as your projects progress.

How to make sense of your journey maps

1. Look deeper.

Depending on the journeys you mapped, making sense of them can take different forms. But as a rule of thumb, we always need to probe deeper into why the customer behaved a certain way or felt a certain way. The emotional curve, especially, always calls for further inquiry.

When we mapped the journeys of an executive course registration process, most maps had a positive wave of emotion when people received the confirmation email from the university. On the surface, there didn't seem to be anything wrong with the process, or with the email. But when we dug deeper into the customers' verbatim quotes, we found some intriguing insights.

Let's compare two journey maps. The line graph traces the rise and fall of people's emotions along the journey of applying for the course, starting from when the thought of attending such a course first arose. Both maps show the curve rising to a highly positive emotional state at the point of receiving the confirmation email.

For some people, this was because **it signalled the beginning of an exciting experience**. Looking at the early stages of the first journey map, we see that this busy professional was looking forward to taking some days off work to immerse herself into new topics.

For other people, attending the course was a mandatory training requirement, and the registration process had been administratively troublesome. **The course confirmation email therefore signified the end of a painful process.** When we probed further, the user represented in the second journey map actually mentioned that the confirmation email wasn't necessarily well done, and there was room for improvement in the orientation process on the first day.

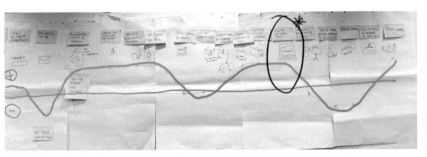

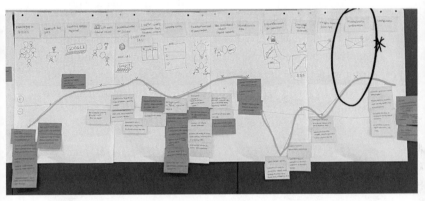

By reading deeper into the emotional curve, we were thus able to derive a whole host of interesting insights, including:

1. Attending a course held a variety of meanings for these professionals. These meanings could have been used to strengthen the value proposition of the programme, or to explore differentiation strategies.

2. The confirmation email is such an important moment in the process. Instead of thinking they were doing well enough in this aspect, the team could further refine this step of the journey to create a really memorable experience. This takes us to the next point: amplifying the positive moments.

2. Don't forget to look at positive peaks too.

When analysing journey maps, teams tend to zoom in on the "pits" – the negative moments – and immediately discuss how to fix them. While it is of course important to do so, we must be careful not to focus exclusively on the negative moments. To design a better customer experience, amplifying the positive moments is just as important.

When we mapped the journey of a family man, who was expecting his first child, in the process of buying a car, the team found a somewhat contradictory moment. The man had quite a negative experience comparing different car options and inter-acting with car dealers. In fact, he said, the service wasn't good. But when he finally signed on the dotted line, his emotional curve went up to positive.

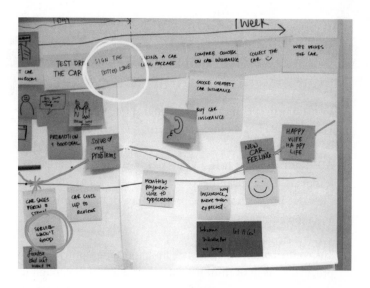

We saw the same pattern in other people's stories of buying a car or home – no matter how difficult or frustrating the process might have been, there would be a clear surge of positive emotions when signing the contract.

When the team dug deeper, we learned that what drove this positive emotional surge was a sense of accomplishment. Buying a car or house is a life milestone. Before his family welcomed their first baby, the father-to-be successfully managed to buy a car that would soon take the whole family on many trips together. Signing on the dotted line evoked a great sense of accomplishment and anticipation.

The team went on to discuss opportunities to further enhance the experience: How might we celebrate this special moment? What role could the contract form play in amplifying this moment? How might we design a sales process that resonated with customers' life priorities? So many new possibilities for strengthening the customer relationship grew out of this inquiry.

3. Identify defining moments based on your context.

Chip and Dan Heath, authors of *The Power of Moments*, encourage the idea of identifying defining moments for your brand.[4] **Defining moments refer to meaningful experiences that stand out in our memory.** They argue that companies can proactively create defining moments by incorporating one or more of the following four elements:

- **Moments of elevation:** Moments that rise above the routine. These make us feel engaged, joyful, amazed, motivated.

- **Moments of insight:** Moments that deliver realisation and transformation.

- **Moments of pride:** Moments that commemorate people's achievements.

- **Moments of connection:** Moments that bond us with others. We feel warmth, unity, empathy, validation.

Here's another way of looking at defining moments. Google developed Micro-Moments[5] to help companies understand consumers' buying decisions in the e-commerce environment. It identifies four gaming-changing moments that really matter in the e-commerce context:

MICRO MOMENTS by Google

I WANT TO
KNOW

I WANT TO
GO

I WANT TO
DO

I WANT TO
BUY

Identify the defining moments relevant to your context, such as the nature of your business, your customers and the competitive landscape. Make it an experience your customers remember.

4. Finish strong.

Our mind has a unique mechanism for remembering experiences. According to Laurie Santos from Yale University, when we remember something, we ignore most of it. And it turns out we make an assessment whether or not the experience was good based only on the extreme moments – the pit, the peak, and the end.[6]

So pay extra attention to designing for a positive experience towards the end of any process in order to finish strong. Because that's how people will remember it – whether it got better or worse at the end.

7.4
Elements of experience design

Now that we have discussed how to understand customers' journeys and make sense of the rich picture of journey maps, let's look at how to design experiences.

The idea of designing "experiences" might be foreign to you. How do we design an experience, when an experience is not just a physical product, like a hairdryer? How do we design an experience when it's complex in nature? As we saw in the journey mapping section, an experience is made up of a sequence of steps (events and actions), various touchpoints and emotions.

First, let me share with you an experience I had, and discuss how this experience was designed.

My first government service experience in Singapore

When I relocated to Singapore in 2010, one of the first experiences I had was visiting the Ministry of Manpower (MOM) to get my employment pass and the dependent passes for my family. Jet-lagged after a 13-hour flight and with restless young children in tow, it probably was the last thing I wanted to do. I dreaded the long waiting time and having to get my kids to behave in a government office.

So before we headed to MOM, I said to them: "Kids, we are going to this government thing to get our passes. It's going to take a long time. I really need you to stay quiet, not to run around. If you behave the whole time, I will buy you an ice-cream when we are done. Got it?"

We arrived at the MOM building in this tense frame of mind, but to my complete surprise, the experience was nothing close to what I had imagined.

We stepped into a building with nice open spaces and plenty of daylight. A friendly service staff helped us get a ticket and led us to a waiting area which overlooked the beautiful Singapore River. On the window, there were stylish illustrations of landmarks like the Supreme Court and Marina Bay Sands. Being new to Singapore, I enjoyed learning this interesting information.

When it was our turn, we were shown to an inviting family corner, which had a lovely children's play corner. While my kids were happily occupied playing with the toys, I could go through the process with a relaxed mind. The entire process was straightforward and pleasant, and took only a short time to complete, not hours, as I feared. If I had known, I wouldn't have needed to promise my children ice-cream for behaving!

I don't remember how long it took exactly. What remained strongly is how pleasurable and delightful the whole experience was. It gave me such a great first impression of Singapore – as a thoughtful, empathetic and efficient nation.

When my pass arrived, I also marvelled at the clarity of the letter content and friendly visual design. From the design of physical spaces to service processes and communications material, the Singapore government had created a lovable experience for me and my family.

Great experiences do not happy by accident. They are the result of empathy-based design.

A few years later, I met some of the people who were behind the scenes making this experience with MOM happen. I learned that it was the outcome of rigorous design efforts that started with a deep empathy for people.

Tasked with revamping the customer experience, the project team consisting of MOM officers and designers from IDEO had immersed themselves in the role of users going through the actual process of obtaining an employment pass. They documented in a video the entire journey, from getting a letter containing instructions, to finding the way to MOM, navigating the building, locating the right counter, waiting, and receiving the pass.

The video showed the experience of a man going through the existing process. The viewer can see how confused and disoriented the man is throughout.

For example, while trying to locate the building, the sign he sees says "MOM". He's unsure if he's at the right building. For Singaporeans it is obvious that MOM stands for Ministry of Manpower, but for most foreigners, the acronym doesn't mean anything. Does it mean the word "mom", like mother?

Another scene shows the man having to press a button to get his queue ticket. But he is faced with multiple buttons on the button console. The buttons are labelled, but many of the labels are acronyms he doesn't recognise. He anxiously guesses which button to press and starts waiting. The space he is waiting in is jammed with rows of chairs, with cold electronic signs flashing the queue number.

When the team shared this video with the senior management, it was clear that they needed to radically change the way they designed their services. After many rounds of prototyping the spaces, processes and touchpoints such as letters, a whole new experience was created. And I was one of the beneficiaries of that incredible effort.

Pete Overy, who led this project as a managing director at IDEO at that time, shares how they designed such a delightful experience while dealing with complexity:

"Being human-centred is inherently reductive in nature; by the simple act of observation without judgement, a designer can see distinctions in the experience that most untrained eyes cannot, to support the reframing and design of the elements that make up an experience. In the case of MOM's Employment Pass Services Centre, by asking 'Why not?', we could reframe an opportunity to support a much better outcome for the customers and the costs of running the centre. By considering the potential of being able to control the volume of people we were looking to serve on a given day, and installing an appointment booking system, this simple shift unlocked the opportunity to redesign the entire service, changing the process, reducing the number of counters, defining new roles. As a result, we could also utilise more of the space to create zones for families."

The four elements of experience design

As Pete Overy shared, designing an experience involves more than redesigning a process. Your journey mapping might have revealed that we never experience a single channel alone. Even if you are designing a digital product (e.g. an app), or a process (e.g. a new procurement process), do look for opportunities to design the *whole* experience. My colleague Huang Zi Leong, who was also a designer at IDEO, suggests a simple reminder of the four elements of human experience as a guide for designing experiences:

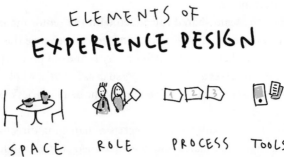

Space
Space refers to physical space that a brand owns, such as offices, shops or branches. (It can also be a public space.) The redesigned Employment Pass Services Centre stands in stark contrast with how it used to look. This friendly, welcoming space creates a strong impression of how government services support foreigners who choose Singapore as a destination to live, work and set up businesses in.

People
People play an important role in delivering experiences. Just as the friendly staff at the Employment Pass Services Centre and their guidance made my day, from the front-line to the back-office, their role has an impact on the customer experience. At the same time, these roles can be redesigned or new ones can be created to deliver a desired experience.

Process

Process refers to steps that enable the desired experience to occur, such as the application process for the employment pass. Companies usually operate based on predefined processes, but negative customer experiences happen not only because the process has not been followed, but mainly because the process itself wasn't designed from the customers' point of view. The key, then, is to relook the process from the customers' point of view through research or journey mapping.

Tools

Tools are things that are designed to help enrich the experience, such as apps, brochures, physical props, etc. In my MOM experience, the letter I received from MOM was so clear, it made a big difference.

You may not need all four of these elements to create an experience, but by expanding your mind using these four elements, you will be able to identify fresh opportunities for creating a simple, enjoyable experience that leaves a long-lasting impression. When a service is well-designed, it can delight people and improve their lives, as the MOM experience did for me. Creating a lovable experience is the result of empathising with customers, addressing each moment of their journey with care, and orchestrating the elements of experience – space, people, process and tools.

Aesthetics matter

Aesthetics is the pleasure all humans derive from perceiving an object or experience through our senses. The Japanese tea room embodies the aesthetic aspect of simplicity. It relaxes us, enhances the sensory experience of being in the moment – seeing, conversing, smelling, tasting, breathing and appreciating beauty.

What part does aesthetics play in achieving simplicity?

The look is the message.

A well-designed space, product, form or website tells customers something quietly:

> "I respect your time. So I prepared the important information for you to consider."

> "You are valued, and I am very interested in doing business with you. Everything we present here is carefully crafted to be clear and make you feel good."

On the other hand, ugly or overcomplicated visuals convey a different message:

"Well, you are just one of many customers. I don't care if you understand this or not. Just fill it out."

Visuals convey a message before people even begin to read or use the actual product. And it moulds customers' perceptions and impressions of your brand.

The look is the function.

A study by Nielsen Norman Group[7] has shown that when something is aesthetically pleasing, it improves people's ability to use and understand it. Consider two mobile banking apps that offer the same features. The aesthetically pleasing one intuitively makes people use the app in a more efficient and effective way compared to the uglier app. The likelihood of users performing wrong transactions is significantly lower.

Aesthetics are the new competitive advantage.

Pauline Brown, a leader in the luxury goods sector, demonstrates in her book, *Aesthetic Intelligence*, how companies who sharpen their ability to make art, create beauty and forge deep human connections win today's and tomorrow's market. She further shares compelling evidence that feelings, not analytic thinking, drive an estimated 85% percent of buying decisions.[8]

As technology advances, the competitive advantage of producing better features and functionalities is getting extremely thin; the new game is to develop the aesthetic advantage. Learning from the consumer retail industry, digital-based products and service-based companies should be rethinking their offerings as lovable experiences.

Designing a sensorial experience

By Dr Tiia Maekinen

Tiia is a leading expert in brand experience at Musta Experience. Among her groundbreaking work was the award-winning sensory concept for Credit Suisse's retail branches in Switzerland. Most of all, Tiia is an inspiring designer practising simplicity in all aspects of her life. I asked her to share how companies can better understand and embrace sensory experience design to build stronger brand perception.

What is sensory experience design?

Just as children learn through the senses, the way we as adults gather information and formulate our analysis of the surroundings is based on sensory experiences. At present, however, sensory experience is rarely more than a clumsy afterthought to experience design. True sensory experience design uses our five human senses to create a holistic, multidimensional and emotionally engaging experience.

Is it possible for a brand to design a specific sensory experience and position itself with it? In my doctoral thesis, I studied different brands and their sensory design and consumers' reactions. It was evident that consumers used their sensory experiences to analyse the various brands and decide whether they liked or disliked a brand. Certain brands had distinct sensory experiences strongly linked to their brand image. For instance, Coca Cola's strongest sensory experience was surprisingly not taste but touch – in the shape and feel of the bottle. Based on my research, I was able to conclude that the senses play a vital role when it comes to building brand awareness and enhancing positive brand image. It is clear that brands should be looking into discovering what are their sensory strengths and weaknesses, and using this knowledge to build their differentiation and positioning strategies.

Multi-sensory design for Credit Suisse

I led a sensory concept design for Credit Suisse's 200 retail branches throughout Switzerland. Our goal was to design a premium experience for customers through the senses, as well as emotionally supporting the customer in the experience. We collaborated with designers and sense experts to develop a concept that took into consideration a complete sensory experience.

For the scent experience, after conducting many tests at various pilot branches with customers and employees alike, we were able to define the best possible scent experience: a fresh scent at the entrance and a brand signature scent to be used as a refreshing spray in the meeting rooms.

For the haptic experience (touch), we focused on finishing materials and furniture selection. For instance, we designed solid leather table covers where customers needed to sign papers, so as to enhance the pleasantness and warmth of the experience.

The visual experience was very much related to the colours we used in the branches as well as decorative elements which drew and delighted the eye, for instance in waiting areas. Additionally, lighting was something we paid a lot of attention to, to ensure smooth and functional customer experience.

For the sound experience, we worked with professional sound designers who developed a 24/7 soundscape for the branch, taking into consideration the time of the day and energy levels of customers and employees.

The main challenges we faced were technical, as most of the sensory experiences needed rather sophisticated delivery systems and hence a lot of onsite support and maintenance. Otherwise, we had very good response from employees and customers alike during the process. This was in 2007, and the innovativeness of the concept was rather striking.

Sensory experiences in the digital world

It has been said by many great designers that details are not just details, details make the experience. This applies equally to designing digital experiences. In particular, we should be looking at designing beyond functionality and usability, and bringing rich sensory experiences to the digital space.

Touch, for instance, relates to motion and the haptics of the experience. These play an important role in the overall ease and simplicity of the experience. As for sound, acoustic experiences in the digital world are so important. Sound can easily become noise, a source of stress for users. However, there are some great examples of how a digital experience can create a relaxing experience. For instance, Calm, a meditation app, allows you to customise the sensory experience of the app to respond to your current mood and needs.

Apart from the five senses, there are our vestibular and proprioceptive systems to take into account. These sensory systems are associated with body movement and balance. Our proprioceptive system provides information to our brain about our body's position in relation to our environment (which direction we are facing, for example, or how close we are to obstacles). It also tells us the amount of effort being used to move our body, and regulates both emotional responses and sensory input. When we think about VR experiences or motion-based digital experiences, understanding these sensory systems is essential for designing with intention.

As the world becomes more digitalised, embracing opportunities to design a sensory experience will give your brand a competitive edge. The key to success is to stay true to the brand, stay consistent, and remember that less is more.

Heighten your design sensitivity

To embrace aesthetics as your strategic asset, you will need to heighten your design sensitivity. You are most likely to use your sense of aesthetics in your personal life (e.g. when choosing clothing or furnishings), but maybe not in the business environment. We may think it's OK that a form looks unpleasant, because it's just a form. We may think it's OK to offer an app that's not beautiful, because it's supposed to be a serious business app. But it's not true. Our products and services need to be designed to go beyond functional needs to win today's consumers.

Human beings love beautiful things. It's in our nature. Bring your sense of aesthetics to work and embody it as an approach to designing customer experiences. Aesthetics matter in your innovation endeavour as they convey the value and worth of your product, your service, your brand. And it starts with conscious awareness and heightening individuals' design sensitivity.

Can bankers learn visual design?

When I was running a design training programme for bankers in OCBC Bank, I included visual design in the curriculum as a fun experiment.

I introduced basic visual design concepts such contrast, flow and balance, and demonstrated how these elements could be used to create a completely different look and feel. The bankers then had the opportunity to became graphic designers for a day. They played with these elements, produced new visual design solutions and shared their designs in front of the group. It was an eye-opening exercise for me as well as the participants to speak the language of design and to see the massive improvements in the outcomes.

When I reviewed the feedback of the training, to my surprise, the visual design section came up as one of the most valuable parts of the training. The participants wanted to learn more and to apply these new ideas in their day-to-day work. Some participants said that being aware of the basics of visual design gave them a completely new perspective in looking at things!

Good design doesn't necessarily cost more. When people are empowered with the basics of visual design, their design sensitivity is heightened, and they are able to make better design decisions in any situation.

Visual design principles for simplicity

Visual design and achieving simplicity are tightly connected. Creating effective visual design requires expertise, knowledge and lots of practice. Contrary to the common belief that a good aesthetic sense is inborn, it is actually learnable. That's because we human beings have a natural appreciation for beauty. We just need to awaken our inner nature and make mindful aesthetic decisions. Just as we seek beauty in our personal lives, we can do the same in business.

Here are the four most fundamental building blocks of visual design, which will have you seeing and thinking like a designer.

1. Contrast

Contrast refers to the differences in size or colour that make an object or image distinguishable. In visual design, contrast is used to get people to look where you want them to look. Use contrast to give emphasis to the most important element.

Let's say there are nine doors. How would you create contrast?

We can do that by using a different **colour**:

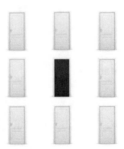

By making it bigger, in other words, **size**:

By creating a **distance**:

By **grouping**:

By changing **orientation**:

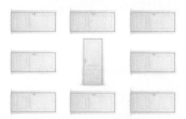

Visual designers are masters of using contrast to create visual emphasis and hence draw users' attention to the most important information. By being aware of different ways to create contrast, we can achieve visual simplicity using just a few graphic elements.

2. Visual hierarchy

Visual hierarchy is the *logic* behind a visual design. It controls the delivery and impact of a message.[9] The best example of visual hierarchy would be a book's table of contents.

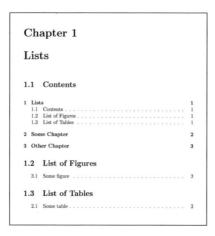

The differences in font size and font weights, as well as the different levels of indenting, give us an understanding of how the content is structured – at one glance.

In the example below, the screen on the left has no visual hierarchy. What's the most important function here? It's hard to tell. We're presented with three large buttons, the "back" button being the most prominent!

 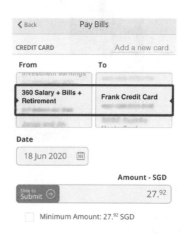

The screen on the right, however, has one large button that stands out: "Slide to submit". This is the primary task of this screen, and therefore deserves the strongest visual emphasis. The secondary task, "Add new card" is there, but it has less visual emphasis. The recovery tasks such as "Back" are positioned away from the centre of the screen in order not to distract users from getting their main task done, while remaining available if needed.

Here's another example. In the poster below, the principles of contrast and visual hierarchy have been applied to organise a large amount of content. The design uses different font sizes and weights to establish a visual order and guide readers through the content, while using unfussy graphic elements to achieve simplicity.

3. Flow

Flow is what guides users to look at things or use functions in a certain order.

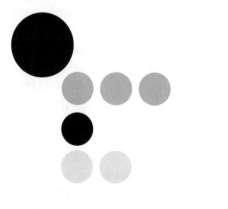

When you look at the image above, where do your eyes start looking and how do your eyes move? Most likely you started from the big circle in the top left, followed by the cluster of circles in the middle and finally to the bottom right.

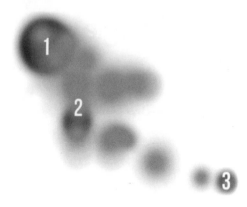

That's because the image was designed to guide you to read it in precisely that sequence, by using size, colour, spacing and grouping. Visual hierarchy is key in creating order and meaning in the midst of complexity. This idea needs to be applied in all aspects of touchpoints such as systems or app design to help users through the process smoothly. Think about your content in terms of primary and secondary, and give visual emphasis accordingly.

4. White space

Originating in the aesthetics of Zen Buddhism, simplicity in Japanese design is achieved by using white space, or negative space. The great expanses of negative space contrast with the positive elements to give the viewer a focal point.[10]

Google does it best with their homepage. There is the Google logo, the search bar and the submit buttons (plus language options depending on where you are). That's all. The rest is a great expanse of white space. They could be using all this space to sell ads. But they don't.

Since Google's beginnings as primarily a search engine, they have grown to offer a bewildering array of services. But they've kept their homepage design as simple and uncluttered as Day One. Their mission of making information accessible and useful is beautifully expressed through the visual design of their homepage.

White space is not a waste. It's about giving important information the attention it deserves. I've seen some forms that try to cram as much information as possible on one page. Yes, you managed to fit everything on a single page, but the information is so packed that users don't know where to begin.

By introducing white space, you may end up using more pages than before, but it is visually far more inviting, friendly and clear. So whether you're designing screens for digital tools or printed materials, use white space strategically to give your content adequate breathing room, emphasise what's important, and create visual focus.

———

Obsess with aesthetics. Because simplicity is an aesthetic experience. Heighten your design sensitivity and use the basic rules of visual design for everything you create, from forms, documents, digital tools to physical space. Nothing is too detailed in creating a lovable experience.

Digitising wealth management services

All projects have their own challenges and complexity. Implementing a new initiative is never a straightforward process. But in hindsight, we can draw some lessons: What drove us forward? What really made a difference?

In this section, I would like to walk you through one project – a digital wealth management service launched as OCBC One-Wealth in 2016 – through the lens of the Simplicity Diamond, to show you how the principles of simplicity were applied.

The problem statement

Changes in customer behaviour and expectations in wealth management

In the old days, building a strong relationship with a customer was mainly done through bankers (so-called relationship managers) who advised customers on investment ideas and helped them execute. Owing to the advancement of the internet, customers now have better access to information and more avenues for self-managing their financials.

At the same time, the new generation of mass customers demand the same quality of wealth advice and services that used to be offered to high-net-worth customers and are also demanding higher transparency and control. As the traditional relationship model was challenged, it was inevitable for the bank to redefine the wealth management business model, to meet the high expectations of the digitally empowered generation.

The need was urgent. Several of the bank's competitors already had their own digital platforms. Because of the time pressure, there were calls within the organisation to use these competitors' platforms as benchmarks and launch something similar quickly.

Get fuelled by empathy

The team deliberately channelled our efforts into first finding out the customers' perspective – how did they typically go about making investments – as opposed to immediately looking into how to sell them more wealth management products on digital channels.

When we had one-on-one conversations with them to collect stories of how they managed their wealth, one of the key learning points was that the investment journey doesn't start at the point where people want to buy. It is a long, complex process, one that involves multiple stages of information gathering and validation. Customers are interested in growing their wealth and want to be involved in the process of investment, but they are overwhelmed and confused by the range and complexity of investment products and information out there.

Furthermore, there was the perception among quite a few customers that bankers were only interested in selling, not helping them monitor and grow their money after the sale was done. One of the memorable quotes during the customer interviews was: "My banker calls me to advise me to buy a product. But I've never received a call from him saying, 'It's time to sell.'"

Looking at their experiences and pain points, we were inspired to see the problem differently. Our initial objective – building a platform to sell products digitally – wouldn't be the right approach. What we had to address was the complexity, and look at how to help customers build confidence throughout the investment process. With this reframing, everything changed.

Dance with complexity

To take on this mission of building confidence in our customers, we needed to work with an army of people to simplify the entire process, including existing processes such as financial needs analysis. We worked with stakeholders from advisors, product experts, technology and operations to legal and compliance, in order to come up with creative solutions to make the journey as simple as possible for the customers. The meeting room was filled with visualisations of the current process, and prototypes of all kinds. We relentlessly tested, and when we encountered problems, we iterated again.

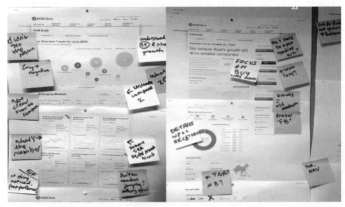

Evolving the idea through prototyping and testing

Focus

This was our focus statement (introduced in Chapter 5), which required many meetings to come up with, but which helped us stay focused on our *why* whenever we were tempted to add more features:

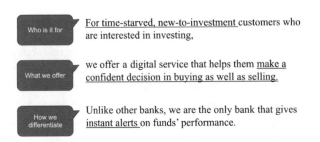

One of the key changes we made, which was quite controversial among the stakeholders, was to massively reduce the number of products on offer. We believed that offering fewer but better products with conviction would help people make better decisions, as opposed to offering a lot of products, which our competitors were doing at that time.

We also lowered the minimum investment amount to as low as S$100. This allowed customers to start small and then gradually build up as they gained confidence. First-time investors do not want to risk investing a lot of money before they understand what they're getting into. Investors can now access up-to-date market information on their mobile devices, and all the research content is curated and bite-sized, written in plain English without jargon.

While a lot of effort has been put into helping customers buy investments, it is also crucial to support customers in making confident selling decisions. We designed two ways of doing this: (1) Users can set an alert to get informed on the performance of their investments, so they can take the necessary actions in a timely manner. (2) Personalised alerts based on our data analytics inform users when they need to take any action on the investments they hold.

Speak human

We learned that content such as market outlook reports and investment ideas play a critical role in the investment process. However, this kind of content used to be distributed by newsletters to a selected group of customers, and these were written in a technical way. We had to simplify the content and craft it for a digital reading experience.

We worked with the wealth management content team, who were most enthusiastic about humanising all the research content. This kind of change required much more work of them but they became the great partners who danced with us through the swamp of complex research content and we established a new humanised editorial standard. One of key changes has been using the human voice and avoiding passive verbs. Not only does simplifying the language make the content clearer, it also helps the bank communicate with conviction about a product. Receiving information and advice from a humanised voice, customers feel more empowered and confident to make an informed decision.

Design lovable experiences

Integrating digital and people

Designing digital tools doesn't mean we are eliminating the role of humans. In fact, it became an opportunity to strengthen our relationship managers' role and to enhance the cross-channel experience.

We had observed that customers had different preferences in choosing between digital platforms and the human touch. Some liked to start their journey online, but when it came to execution they preferred meeting a real person for support and validation. Some preferred their first point of contact to be their relationship manager, yet after thinking about the investment ideas suggested by the relationship manager, they would execute at their own convenience over a digital channel. And of course there were also some who felt very comfortable doing everything on their own.

We thus looked at crafting a seamless experience across all channels from digital to physical and vice versa. For example, after suggesting an investment product idea, the digital channel would ask if users wanted to speak to someone for more advice. To make this feature work, we made sure the digital channel was linked to branch manpower to trigger timely contact by an advisor. Or, when customers met their relationship managers, the relationship managers could encourage them to make a decision in their own time, and take the opportunity to introduce the digital app. The digital sales would then be recognised under the relationship manager who had been advising the customer.

Simplify to build confidence

Get informed ·············*Consider* ·············*Buy* ·············*Manage*

Designing a pleasurable digital experience

Putting it all together, we wanted our intent of designing for confident investment decisions to be visualised. We wanted to create a relaxed and pleasurable experience through effective visual design. We used images for featured articles, provided ample white space, and set clear visual hierarchies. The colours, typefaces and images were deliberately selected to achieve the objective.

By orchestrating elements of experience such as content, product, channel and data analytics towards simplicity that helps people make confident investment decisions, the tool became far more powerful than just an investment platform that sells products online.

The result of simplicity

Soon after its launch, the digital tool was generating more than 60% of the total transaction volume, and sales grew strongly. Close to 70% of those who use this tool bought an investment for the first time and went on to purchase multiple funds after that. This shows investors gaining confidence.

Aditya Gupta, Senior Vice-President of OCBC, and my partner-in-crime on this project, said that the convergence of digital technologies and simplicity can make quality wealth management advice and solutions more accessible and inclusive for all customers. It results in democratising wealth management, which helps companies expand the wealth advice market and unlock new consumer segments – e.g. emerging affluent, millennial, first-time investors – who have traditionally never had access to quality wealth management services.

If we had focused on "how to innovate our digital platform", the outcome would have been very different. Innovation happens when we get closer to the heartbeat of users and understand the barriers from their perspective, not in following your competitors or tech trends. That's ultimately what gave the team a competitive edge in building new digital capabilities.

Part III
Make it happen

We should not assume that simplicity always depends on major changes. Slight changes in small things can sometimes make things much simpler.
— Edward De Bono

PART III IS DEDICATED TO practitioners, who are doing the work of bringing people together and driving change.

Implementing simplicity in an organisation is hard. Organisations are complex, and people are resistant to change. So it's going to take more than knowing the concepts and methods you've learned so far. The real game depends on developing soft skills and leadership, to get the people in your organisation on the same page and drive momentum towards tangible change.

Part III is inspired by questions I've gathered from conference audiences globally and my executive students who are change agents in their organisations. These are the very real issues that people face in implementing simplicity. The questions often boil down to three main themes: starting the simplicity journey; influencing people; and scaling the simplicity movement. We'll discuss each of these themes in the three following chapters.

Chapter 8. How to start
8.1   How do we start the simplicity journey?
8.2   What kind of people do we hire to build a team?

Chapter 9. How to influence people
9.1   How do we get stakeholders' buy-in?
9.2   How do we move "the middle"?

Chapter 10. How to change culture and scale
10.1   Establish organisation-wide design principles
10.2   Design your physical space to reflect your intent
10.3   Change the vocabulary
10.4   Design the new working model
10.5   Empower people with the skillset and mindset
10.6   Implementing a simplicity program at a large company

Chapter 8
How to start

How do we start the simplicity journey?

You've just been tasked with a big initiative. It could be in the realm of digital transformation, customer-centricity or innovation. You might have a team, or you might need to build a new team. You are probably excited and pumped up by this new mission. At the same time, you might be feeling overwhelmed as to where to start.

Before starting anything out of excitement, make sure you are set up for success. Ensure that you have the key ingredients first.

1. Demand these first.

Mandate

First and foremost, obtain your mandate. What is your role supposed to deliver? What is the desired outcome? Discuss with your sponsor or boss to have your mandate clearly articulated and communicated in the organisation.

A mandate is like having a licence. James Bond can complete his cool missions because he's got a licence to kill. Perhaps using James Bond as an example is a bit dramatic, but having a clear mandate is crucial for starting the simplicity journey.

Personally, my division's clear mandate given by the bank's CEO (to differentiate the bank through customer experience) gave me a licence to advocate customers' perspective and to challenge certain business decisions. Sometimes the licence was used to kill a project if wasn't going to create value for customers. You need a mandate to do the right thing, even if it takes more time to launch.

Seat

Seat refers to the power needed to influence a decision. Every organisation has a body such as a steering committee – a group of representatives who are part of the decision-making process for a given initiative. You or your group function head must have a seat in there. If this seat is not given, it will be very difficult to achieve the desired outcome.

Structure

Managing change requires structure. Structure includes the process and the game plan. If you can influence it, this also needs to include the organisational structure. There is no one formula for the "best" organisational structure in driving change, but based on my experience and observations, it is particularly effective when the innovation group reports directly to the CEO or COO, and the group has independence from other groups or channels. The idea is to allow "creative tension" between the business-as-usual and the new force.

An innovation group should be placed close to the business to drive change, rather than being a think tank group. To create real immediate impact and to maximise the learning, working with the business units and solving current real-life problems have to be a key part of their job scope.

2. Look for quick wins.

People need to see and feel the difference when change is happening. Identify quick-win opportunities where you can show the value of simplicity.

In the first year of OCBC Bank's design journey, the team looked for quick wins in redesigning the paper forms that were placed in the branches and used by customers for transactions such as payments, account opening, change of address, buying a product, etc.

For example, take the "change of address" form. More than 20% of forms were filled incorrectly. Customers either missed out some mandatory fields, or they did not fill it out correctly. Would you blame the customers for not being able to fill out a form? Or did the two-digit error rate suggest that the form had inherent problems?

When we redesigned the form to be easy to understand and visually clean, the number of customers who filled it out wrongly was reduced from 20% to less then 1%. This benefited the business by reducing the operational effort. After just two months, the team was able to demonstrate the value of good design.

This kind of before-and-after is powerful for mobilising people in the organisation as well as motivating the team. While you tackle bigger initiatives, which may take a longer time, identify these quick-win opportunities and create small successes along the way.

You can use the Simplicity Diamond to identify opportunities for quick wins. A Korean bank I worked with improved their customer experience by starting with the "Speak human" principle. During my workshop with them, they identified an immediate opportunity for simplification and formed a project team to redesign the communications materials of their key financial products. Within two weeks of intensive work, they massively simplified the product brochures. The redesigned brochures were much more effective in helping advisors introduce the financial products to customers, and for this the team received a standing ovation from the senior management. This quick win inspired both the team and the senior stakeholders to simplify other products and processes, launching them on their simplicity journey.

Create an impact from the quick win and plan for the next impact. This is a better strategy for many organisations. You don't need to make big changes in order to start the journey. You can start with a small project like the Korean bank, learn from it, measure the results and communicate your findings through storytelling. Then expand into building further simplicity capacities wherever the impact will be most powerful.

3. Start where the suction is.

Successful change depends on the people in the organisation. There are people who are naturally curious and passionate about change by design. I would call these people the "suction". Find this suction and work with them.

In the first two years of my team's design journey at OCBC, the wealth management department was the suction for us. We could feel the curiosity and energy of the head of department, and we prioritised our resources to support their business units. The speed and energy of transformation was impressive. The department soon adopted prototyping and co-creation as problem-solving methods, using whatever tools they had in the office (such as paper and PowerPoint) to visualise their ideas. The product managers learned how to meet customers to test their ideas before launching a product. Design became part of their language in their daily practice.

What kind of people do we hire to build a team?

Hire designers.

By designers, I mean people who have an educational background in design disciplines such as graphic, product, industrial or interaction design. While the terminology of these disciplines may change as design schools evolve their curriculum to respond to the changing world, **my definition of designers here refers to people who are trained to build something tangible**.

Why are designers so vital to your team?

1. **Designers are trained to solve problems from the users' perspective.** Designers have natural empathy for users. Their design education equips them with a user-centric mindset and tools.

2. **They connect dots.** Traditional design training such as sketching trains designers' brains to synthesise what they see and distil the essence in their drawings. They also have the fantastic ability to visualise solutions in their head. This accelerates the innovation process by closing the gap between research and execution.

3. **They build prototypes to learn and improve.** They make ideas tangible by building prototypes, allowing you to test with customers, learn and improve quickly.

What kind of design background should they have?

That depends on your team's needs and your scope of mandate. But the one important thing is that you should look for "T-shape" designers. The "T" describes the distribution of traits within the designer: the vertical line represents a deep expertise in a particular design discipline, while the horizontal line represents a breadth of character that encompasses passion, empathy, communication and people skills.

For example, one of my team members has exceptional skills in visualising ideas. She has a great sense of aesthetics, is up-to-date with design trends and able to produce elegant visual solutions. Another member is a master of crafting physical things. He has a deep understanding of different materials and can produce ergonomic design solutions for physical spaces. And they both possess natural empathy for users and constantly ask themselves how their designs can be improved to better support these users.

Do they need to have industry knowledge?

It can help, but it's not absolutely necessary. In fact, the fresher they are to your industry, the more effective they may be in simplicity work, as they are likely to see things with fresh eyes. Their "naive" questions are valuable sources for simplification.

But in order for their skills to reach their full potential, designers need to be developed and supported. Develop their soft skills such as communications and people management. Today, the designer's role has become one of a change agent. It is imperative for them to mobilise the people in their organisations to lead customer-centricity. Place them in the right structure, where they can be involved in the early stages of innovation and strategic discussion.

Chapter 9
How to influence people

How do we get stakeholders' buy-in?

Achieving simplicity is a team sport. We need to learn how to "dance" with people from different departments, as we discussed in Chapter 4. We need support from subject matter experts. And we need the endorsement of senior management, especially when systemic changes are involved.

The question is, how do we get stakeholders' and senior management's buy-in in the process? I have addressed this throughout the book, but here I want to bring together the key elements to show you just how it can be done.

1. Encourage empathy.

Involve your stakeholders early, starting from the research phase. When conducting interviews with customers, for example, invite your stakeholders to observe. Create an environment where they can see and hear what users have to say. Direct observation of what users do engenders empathy, and is very powerful in driving change. Much more effective than any research report.

Some stakeholders may say they don't have time to join. Ask them to attend one session (keep it to 1 hour max). After observing users directly, I tell you, this person will want more.

2. Prototype with your stakeholders.

Prototyping is not only a designer's tool. It's a powerful *thinking* tool for visualising and testing ideas. Involve your stakeholders by inviting them to co-create prototypes. Firstly, it's visual – it creates a shared understanding of the situation. Secondly, it's hands-on, and they will be naturally more engaged in the conversation and solution-building. Then test the prototype with customers while having them as observers.

3. Use your source of power.

We typically assume that the power to influence others comes from holding a position of authority. While it is true that being in a senior position in an organisation can help you drive change, we also need to look beyond that, at broader sources of power:

- **Expertise** is a source of power. If you are an expert in a certain methodology or possess domain knowledge, that gives you power to influence people.

- **Networks** are also a source of power. If you have a good relationship with people in your organisation, it can play a positive role in your ability to influence others.

- **Liking.** If you are one of those who are liked and popular, recognise it as a source of power.

- **Reciprocity.** When you frequently help others solve their problems, or do them a favour, the sense of reciprocity can become a source of power for you.

Identify your own sources of power and use it to influence people. You have more power than you have.

4. Inspire through stories.

Storytelling is a powerful tool for inspiring internal stakeholders as well as customers (as discussed in Chapter 6). Identify opportunities to use stories to connect with them. For instance, you can turn dry PowerPoint slides into a compelling story. Complement your stories with pictures and videos where you can, as engaging all the senses puts the message across vividly and memorably. Because when we are able to tell a moving story, we don't need a formal leadership position to influence people. A story creates power.[1]

Tips for engaging stakeholders through storytelling

- **Connect before persuading:** When I present research findings or propose new ideas, I always give the audience the opportunity to connect with the consumers we interviewed by sharing their profiles, anecdotes and sometimes videos. It may appear to be a trivial thing, but building connection with the audience before trying to convince them is key.

- **Entice the senses:** The more senses are involved, the more effective the outcome will be. Examine possibilities for adding sensory stimuli such as touch, feel, smell and sound to your presentations, not just the usual PowerPoint slides.

- **Be interesting:** This sounds obvious, but what can make you interesting is when you address your audience's interests. Be genuinely interested in your audience.

- **Make people remember:** Leave them with feelings and the specifics. It sounds counterintuitive, but often the more specific the story, the more universal the connections.

- **Leave them feeling hopeful:** We sometimes think that we need to make a situation sound urgent or dire to drive change. However, if you can deliver the same message with the feeling of hope, choose the positive option. Humans tend to respond better to positive commands than negative ones.

- **You don't always need to conclude or provide solutions:** The objective can simply be to help your stakeholders see the need for change. Invite them to think about solutions with you, rather than immediately suggesting what and how to change. This is related to point 3, knowing your audience's agenda and their frame of mind. If you foresee resistance to your ideas, try to understand the context and their agenda and address these points through stories rather than focusing on your own conclusions.

How do we move "the middle"?

Let's accept this fact: People resist change.

That's because change doesn't feel secure. Change requires us to step out of our comfort zone, with all its familiar processes and tried-and-tested solutions. Being part of change seems risky.

We may often hear from the top management that simplicity matters, and that we need to do things differently. In order to make things happen, however, the people in the "middle" – those responsible for executing projects and taking care of day-to-day operations – must want the same thing. Unless they embrace the vision and get mobilised, the vision exists only in the speech of the senior management.

Fortunately, there is another fact: People want to do a good job. People are intrinsically motivated by the positive impact they can make in their lives. Nobody wants to be the incompetent one who spends their work hours on things that don't matter, or the mean one who deliberately hinders their organisation's attempts to do the right thing.

How then do we move the middle?

1. Be aware of tunnel vision.

As change agents, we are susceptible to so-called "tunnel vision". We are so intensely focused on the desired outcome that we don't see what's going on outside this "tunnel", such as how people feel about the change, or if they can even see the same vision. The key in managing the change process is to step back whenever you find yourself becoming too singlemindedly focused on the objective. Look at the people around you who you need to work with to make change happen, and make sure they are all onboard.

2. Take a human-centred design approach.

The human-centred approach doesn't only apply to customers. I encourage you to use it to understand the middle group's deeper needs, motivations and fears. They are people too!

Have you ever thought about what drives them? What does success look like to them? How do they feel about the change? The best way to understand these motivations is to take some time to meet these people individually – over a coffee, or lunch or drinks, whichever is most appropriate. When we are genuinely interested in them, and care about their personal values, they are more likely to understand us and see the vision we see.

3. Speak their language.

The middle group may not be familiar with design concepts. Just as any professional field has its own jargon (think of legal documents or a doctor's note), design thinking comes with its own set of technical terms. When we use words like "empathy", "reframing" or "prototyping" without explaining them to the people we work with, we are creating a mental barrier for them. Be mindful of defining and explaining these terms at the start, or find ways to express the idea in words they will understand.

4. See the middle as part of your team.

I recall one internal team meeting at the bank, where I noticed that the team members were using the words "we" and "they" in an intriguing way. "We" was used to refer to the team – the change agent, the designers, the customer-centric people. "They" was used to refer to stakeholders from other units – the business-centric, timeline-sensitive, not-caring-about-customers people. While no one intended to criticise the other group, the language reflected the deeper perception of the different roles involved.

I also notice this mindset when I interact with my executive students. We seem to have this mental model of two different groups, where one stands for change, and the other stands for the status quo.

Dividing people into such groups is unhealthy and counter-productive in driving change. Change agents shouldn't be either "us" or "them". Our role is to become the glue that brings people together and facilitates the process.

5. Actively facilitate to bring out collective creativity.

Finally, to really get "the middle" on your side, you need to give them a feeling of ownership of the process. To achieve this, use the facilitation techniques introduced in this book (such as visual facilitation, or co-creation) or any other methods within your repertoire to draw out their creativity. Empower them to contribute their creative ideas to the design process. When they feel the excitement that comes with seeing the impact of their ideas on the vision, they will be emotionally involved. Creating that emotional engagement is really the key to effectively moving the middle.

———————

People are innately creative, and intrinsically motivated to make a positive impact in their work. Be empathetic towards them before trying to convince them. Speak to them in their language and make them part of the movement.

Chapter 10
How to change culture and scale

JUST AS DESIGNING a customer experience requires multi-dimensional design efforts, driving cultural change in an organisation needs to be approached with all the design elements in mind. Many cultural programmes or change management programmes focus on "processes" or "methodology". But to drive the desired change, you must go beyond work processes or methodologies, and design for all aspects of human experience. These may include changing the physical spaces and daily vocabulary that people use at work. When people feel the change in their environment, you can engage them to join the movement.

Establish organisation-wide design principles

To drive change beyond the present project, we need to turn our attention to building a culture of design within our organisations. One of the strongest ways to start doing that is to lay down a set of design principles to serve as a guiding light.

A really great book on principles is Stephen R. Covey's *7 Habits of Highly Effective People*. I've read through it from cover to cover multiple times, and one of the lessons that sticks clearly in my mind is this: **There is a set of principles that are permanent, unchanging, and universal in nature, as opposed to values, which are internal and subjective, which may change over time.**

This concept of "principles" was both eye-opening and comforting to me. It comforted me that there would always be a set of rules that would guide me regardless of the situations I found myself in, or regardless of the values I held at any point in time. As I progressed in my career and my personal life, I began to better understand and appreciate what Stephen Covey meant by the universal nature of principles.

Why we need principles in the digital age

There is always a tension between what's urgent and what's important, and this tension is increasing all the time due to the pace of change. The innovation agenda is full, but in many organisations the sense of priority is lacking. Having a set of principles can remind you of the ultimate purpose of your company. It can guide all members of the organisation to do the right thing for consumers and to stay close to the ethos of great customer experience, so that we can be focused rather than distracted by trends or by our competition in this fast-changing digital age.

The OCBC Great Design Principles

OCBC's Great Design Principles came about through a rigorous process of the organisation asking itself some probing questions. We asked ourselves: As an organisation, what is the most important thing to us? If we had to choose a handful of principles, what should they be? What principles are relevant in our current environment? How do we communicate these principles so that people can best understand, internalise and utilise them?

After several months of discussions and iterations, eight "Great Design" principles were born:

THE OCBC ~~GOOD~~ GREAT DESIGN PRINCIPLES

because good is the enemy of great

GREAT DESIGN:

❶ CARES
Design is a way to demonstrate that you care for the people you are designing for. When you design with empathy in mind, people will sense that you care.

❷ IS EASY TO USE
There is beauty when something simply works. Great design respects people's time and effort. By making things as clear as possible, we make their lives easier.

❸ DELIGHTS THE SENSES
Great design should have a sense of aesthetic, wellbeing, joyfulness, richness, honesty, wit – emotions that incite pleasure in the experience we provide.

❹ PROVIDES FOCUS
Users are on a mission. Don't interrupt them or set up obstacles. Great design allows people to focus on their task and complete it quickly.

❺ IS IN THE DETAILS
The difference between good and great is attention to detail. Great experience is the result of carefully orchestrating every single design element, such as content, font, colour, texture and tone of voice.

❻ WRITES CLEARLY
The way we write has become more important with the rise of artificial intelligence and conversational interfaces. Great writing is clear and honest.

❼ PRESENTS FEWER BUT BETTER CHOICES
The more choices people have, the harder it is for them to choose. Great design removes the unnecessary and adds the meaningful to help people make confident decisions.

❽ IS RELEVANT
Always look at the context users are in such as environment, situation and emotional state. By fully understanding the context we can make our product relevant to users.

🟠 OCBC Bank

What's your great design story? Tell us at **design@ocbc.com**

Establishing and communicating these design principles isn't the end, but rather just the beginning. They need to be iterated and internalised by the organisation, so that people at all levels of management are equipped to make the right decisions, to assess situations clearly, and to adapt the technology at hand to best serve the ultimate goals of our customers and our business.

Design your physical space to reflect your intent

Design workspaces to reflect your intent and the kind of culture you want to cultivate. Well-crafted space design can change people's perceptions and their behaviour. Whatever your budget, you will always find design options to achieve your objective. It's really about your intent and mindful design decisions, not about spending a lot of money to make it fancy.

When OCBC's Group Customer Experience team was just formed, we were given an empty office with some generic cubicle-style corporate furniture.

The first thing that David McQuillen, then Head of Group Customer Experience, did was to "donate" his corner office space, which allowed us have a large pantry. He then sat at one of the desks just like everyone else. The pantry, with a fantastic view overlooking the Singapore River, became an energising space for the team to connect informally and share ideas.

The office was designed by Head of Experience Design, Bojan Blecic, a former architect, with the limited budget we had. He created the open space concept, designed themed rooms for important activities such as research and prototyping, as well as inducing creative collaboration through a thoughtful choice of colours and materials.

We bought furniture from IKEA, but did so with clear intent. For example, the meeting rooms were designed for *doing*, rather than sitting down and talking. The whiteboard stretched the entire length of one wall. A large table was placed in the middle of the space. Instead of the standard high-back office chairs with arm-rests commonly found in meeting rooms, we provided stools. The idea was to encourage people to get off their butts as much as possible, move around, make things, get hands-on.

Each room had its own visual theme – tropical rainforest, shophouses, hawker centres – to create typical Singaporean scenes that made us feel close to where our customers were. I took those photos early in the morning to get the best shots, and we used them as wallpaper for each room. And everyone in the team volunteered their time and talents to create a space we loved in every corner and detail.

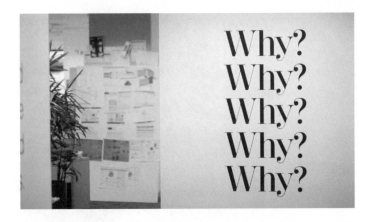

Next, we created a designated space for direct customer research – the Experience Labs (discussed in Chapter 3) – which consisted of an interview room and an observers' room. The interview room was designed to look like someone's living room to create a comfortable atmosphere for customers to open up to us. The observers' room was designed not only to video-stream the interview scenes, but also to maximise active listening. Small tables attached to the seats were deliberately chosen to discourage checking of emails on laptops, and to instead encourage stakeholders to focus on listening and taking notes of their observation.

The Studio, a large, rather raw-looking space, was dedicated to prototyping, workshops and training. Everything in the room was movable and flexible so that the room could be used for various parts of the design process. Sometimes there would be lots of boards showing new app designs. At other times, the space would be filled with furniture prototypes for banking branches.

Very soon, among colleagues and stakeholders, our Group Customer Experience office became a beloved spot to get the creative juices flowing for all kinds of projects.

Designing physical space is a great way to influence the culture of your team and your organisation. People behave in certain ways depending on how the space is designed, what atmosphere it creates. It doesn't need to be expensive. As we did with the Group Customer Experience office, it's all about having an intent and having everyone's creative involvement that reflects the kind of culture you want to cultivate.

Change the vocabulary

Words are powerful. If we can influence the daily vocabulary of the people in our organisation, we can also change their way of thinking. A list of phrases like this will go a long way in infusing a design-oriented mindset across the organisation:

We don't say	We say,
My boss wants me to build this as soon as possible.	We have some **hypothesis**. Let's **talk to customers** to find out.
Brainstorm	**Ideate** based on the insight
Solutions	**Experiment opportunities**
We don't have time. Let's skip design research.	Let's run **The Design Sprint** to find out.
The management already decided that..	Is this **a minimum lovable product** for our customers?

In addition, key concepts such as empathy, journey mapping and storytelling can become the name and theme of meeting rooms, to introduce the language of design and simplicity into the daily dialogue. We also designed a journal booklet with great attention to detail and craftsmanship to accompany the journey.

Look out for these kinds of small opportunities to design the change. These small things can become the mighty force in scaling the new way of thinking.

Design the new working model

Organisations recognise that so-called old ways of working are no longer competitive. Think about an IT process. User requirements are determined by business analysts, then documented by a project manager, then passed to developers, who need to go through the rows and rows of requirements to implement in the system. It's slow and ineffective.

In the digital age, where industries are being disrupted by new entrants, organisations now look to adopt new methods to respond to the need for creativity and speed in designing products and services. You might have heard of or adopted Design Thinking, Lean or Agile methodology. These new methods sound very good in case studies, but they seem to be very hard to implement.

Methods must be experienced, not forced.

There are many reasons why a trendy method is hard to implement. Often it's because such methods are forced on people. Suddenly people are told to fail fast, and launch fast, while the key performance indicator hasn't changed. I've seen organisations become a fast-running machine but solving the wrong problems – because people were just told to be fast.

In introducing new methods, we must emotionally engage people. **Any new innovation methods must be felt and experienced.** When people are engaged emotionally, when they feel the possibility that innovation can be done, this is where acceptance and willingness kick in.

I've designed many training programmes for organisations to introduce new methods and working models. When I design such programmes, what I pay most attention to is to have the participants leave the room with positive and optimistic feelings.

Not that the methods I cover during the training are leisurely or super easy to learn. Participants indeed work very hard. But the training is always designed in a way that they see the connections between the methods, and get to see the fruit of their work – and have a good laugh along the way. Because I believe this is where real change and empowerment happens.

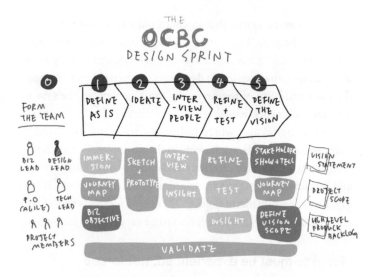

The new working model was designed to maximise empathy and immerse the team in new methods.

Empower people with the skillset and mindset

Turning bankers into design warriors

In the later part of 2017, when the rate of change accelerated in the competitive landscape of the financial services, while planning the strategic direction of the Experience Design team at OCBC, we realised that designing great experiences could not be the job of one department alone. We saw that we had to expand the role of design, to turn all employees into innovators equipped with an empathetic mindset, sensitivity towards simplicity and the tools to drive change.

I developed the OCBC Great Design Programme – an organisation-wide innovation capability building programme – supported by the COO. My awesome colleagues Huang Zi Leong and Jeremy Ng joined this mission, and together we executed the programme and grew the community. With each run, we learned so much, and iterated the content and format of the programme to create bigger impact. Over the course of a year, some 200 business heads and IT managers learnt how to solve complex business problems through an intensive bootcamp programme.

In just a few months, we saw positive results among business units across the organisation. Where bankers used to have little understanding of design, they now actively embraced design methods as a way to innovate. The changes in the way projects were carried out and the outcome were noticed by the respective department heads. The demand for the programme was very high.

Taking a targeted approach

We had to find a way to create the biggest impact possible with the limited resources we had, while keeping this positive momentum going.

*The Great Design Journal was designed to
accompany the bankers' design journey*

Instead of approaching it as "training" where it is hard to measure the outcome and provide support, we married training with an "incubating a project" model. We would identify strategically important projects with the division head, who would provide the problem statement that was being discussed in the boardroom. With their support, a cross-functional team would be formed. From there, Great Design Programme faculty members would custom-design the programme to tackle the specific business problem.

The power of starting it right

Typically the programme starts with training in the design thinking method, and meeting customers. The aim is to create an alignment of methods and to have empathy with customers and users. I've learned that having alignment and empathy provides a solid foundation for any project, no matter how complex it is. It gets people to speak the same language for the rest of the project. The team is then fuelled by empathy to get their creativity juices flowing. Using the Great Design Programme as a project launchpad turned out to be an effective model that brought senior managers and project team members together, and made the innovation process visible and tangible.

Proficiency breeds agility

One of the concerns that companies have in scaling a new method is maintaining agility while taking a customer-centric approach. I have thought about this question a lot, because it seems to be very hard to be customer-centric, doing all the research and testing, and yet launch something fast. Many companies look to Agile methodology to find the answer.

While Agile is a wonderful method, it can be misleading because of its name. To adopt a new method such as Agile successfully, companies must meet certain requirements (such as changing the decision-making model to empower self-managing teams, having the right product owner who can make sound decisions, etc.). Instead of looking for answers in a specific method, I suggest increasing your proficiency in the method you are using or plan to adopt. Master the principles and key methods until it becomes natural to you. When we master a certain way of thinking, we became proficient at it, and we get faster while doing the right thing. *That* is the true agility we need in the era of the innovation imperative.

Implementing a simplicity programme in a large company

By Mark McCormick
Senior Vice President at Wells Fargo

Mark is a man of sharp strategic mind and humility. Since the day we met at a conference in China, we have bonded through simplicity, have grown our passion for driving changes in our organisations. Throughout all these years, we exchanged ideas and thoughts on the challenges of implementing simplicity. His simplicity journey at Wells Fargo – how he created a movement and grew simplicity evangelists – is truly inspiring. I asked him for his story of how he made it happen.

How the journey started

I tell this story a lot, and it usually goes like this. In 2013 I was invited to speak at a conference called Next Bank China. It brought together customer experience leaders and financial services leaders from around the world to talk about the future of banking.

Wells Fargo, where I was working as Head of Digital Customer Experience, enjoys a favourable reputation internationally, for good reason, as being an innovative financial services company. Many banking innovations were started at Wells Fargo, and we continue to invest in finding innovative ways to serve our customers.

I went to China with a good story about how we taught the basic tenets of innovation through a program called Innovation Bootcamp. And I had some powerful demos to show of new products and services we were developing, leveraging some of the newest technologies.

I would add that I was very proud to be invited to speak at this forum, and I was also delighted at the rock-star treatment the conference organizers arranged: first-class plane tickets, fancy hotels, and massive posters of our headshots adorning the conference hall. I have to say, my ego was quite inflated by the time I hit the stage.

Yet, I was completely humbled in every way once Jin Kang Møller took the stage. Luckily she went after me and not before; if it had been reversed, I'm not sure I would have had the will to deliver my message, because Jin's presentation absolutely floored me.

She talked about how the bank where she worked, OCBC Bank of Singapore, was simplifying their most complex customer experiences and communications – and driving great value in doing so. She presented detailed examples and outlined some basic principles like "Speak Human".

Never before had I experienced such a powerful professional epiphany. Simplicity, I saw then, held the only way to unlock value through the customer experience in a financial services company.

All other strategies, like innovation, personalization, and convenience, suddenly seemed hollow to me, unless they were in service to simplicity. And it came to me like a flash that the most successful new startup companies were the ones that made a complex task more simple – getting a ride, for example: Uber and Lyft are much simpler than calling for a cab. Honestly, my focus became very single-minded, because I was convinced that making things simple unlocked value in a way no other strategy could.

I went back to California with a passionate determination to shape and drive an innovation strategy.

Bringing home the message

I started putting some ideas down, naturally in the form of Power-Point slides, and presenting to increasingly large audiences at Wells Fargo. I asked people if they were interested in learning more and helping with research. There was great appetite for exploring this – no surprise, since the idea is easy to grasp and evocative – so I organized a small band of colleagues to help. From then on, everything was teamwork.

We started by diving into all the research we could find. First we looked at secondary market research to discover that organizations like The Corporate Executive Board (now owned by Gartner) and Siegel and Gale, a global brand and design firm, had been studying simplicity for a while; indeed there was quite a bit of data out there to prove that simplicity drives loyalty, while complexity makes people abandon any given customer experience as well as companies.

Moreover, we found that many of the great thinkers in customer experience had been espousing simplicity as a unifying principle, including John Maeda, of MIT (at the time). There were several books that presented various theoretical frameworks and anecdotal evidence demonstrating that customers craved simplicity. In fact, our research took us all the way back to Richard Saul Wurman's *Information Anxiety*.

And we found inspiration from some of the great thinkers, entrepreneurs, and designers of the 20th century, including Steve Jobs, who famously said, "Simple is hard. You have to work hard to make your thinking clean to make things simple." Coco Chanel, whose impact on fashion is still felt, famously asserted that every woman should have at least one little black dress in her closet, but more importantly suggested that the essence of true elegance is simplicity. I got that example from Jin directly, but it became a crowd-pleaser when we finally started presenting this material.

In other words, we didn't limit our research to financial services. Far from it. We believed then, and still do, that customers' expectations for simple experiences are being driven by experiences they are having in other industries, like hospitality and electronics.

Had we limited our research to banking, there would have been no end of complex experiences begging to be simplified. We cited Alan Siegel, who gave a great TED talk where he proved that a credit card's terms and conditions pamphlet (usually running to dozens of pages with small print and unintelligible prose) could actually be reduced to one page *and* be cleared by the ever-vigilant legal, risk, and compliance attorneys he consulted. All of our research culminated in a few things.

First, through many, many iterations, we built a three-part framework with fundamental principles for making things simple:

1. Commit to the essentials

2. Create a human story

3. Iterate, test and measure

Each of these principles had strategies, and each strategy had tips, tricks and tools.

Underlying all of these principles was a more lofty unifying philosophy: empathy. To make things simple for others, you first have to connect with a part of yourself that craves simplicity. We demonstrated this by sharing stories of our own battles with things like too much choice, which, research shows, is perceived by people as signalling complexity. For example, I talked of the extensive array of granola at my corner grocer: 67 different varieties! Too much choice. Sheena Iyengar of course proved that consumers don't actually buy anything at all when faced with too much choice.

Then we set out to change the company.

Starting a movement

One of the early decisions was to create a full-day immersive experience with three objectives:

1. Communicate the background and case for change

2. Teach the framework experientially and create opportunities to practice making things more simple

3. Create more simplicity evangelists

We realized that if we were asking people to invest a whole day, we needed to make sure the experience was of the highest quality, both experientially and pedagogically. So we turned to a trusted partner, Humantific, a boutique firm out of New York City whose value proposition is "navigating complexity". I had worked with them on several occasions to create full-day learning experiences.

They immediately saw the synergies between what we were trying to do and the fundamentals of creative problem-solving, which is now commonly referred to as "design thinking". Indeed, simplicity principles and practices are not that much different from what's known variously as "creative problem solving", "human-centered design", or "design thinking". In some ways, we were creating a new dialect of an old language, but one that promised to demystify those methodologies and be applicable to both very small-scale operational nits as well as large-scale transformations.

To generate interest in the full-day program, we put together a 40-minute "roadshow" that we presented at as many team meetings as we could. The roadshow presented the basic business case for simplicity and featured many inspiring examples of companies that were gaining market attention for their simple solutions to complex problems. We kept driving home the point that innovation was not gadgetry or electronic solutions; innovation was making something simpler.

We demonstrated that people craved simplicity in three ways: practically, intellectually and emotionally.

People started signing up for workshops in droves. And those that came talked about the experience to their colleagues, who in turn signed up. Pretty soon we were running two flavors of workshops: "open enrollment", which was open to anyone and featured general examples, and "bespoke" – these were customized workshops for different lines of business. We would work beforehand with the business leaders to gather particular problems they were facing and feature those examples in the workshop.

Seeing results

My own career morphed at that point as I took a position in a strategic design department. That group was nestled in a larger business process team, and the head of that group was a very analytical and wise individual. He loved the program and realized that we needed to start tracking some metrics in order for it to perceived as worthy of continued investment.

So we built a dashboard and started tracking key quantitative and qualitative progress indicators of The Simplicity Project. We tracked the number of requests we were getting, the NPS ratings on post-workshop surveys, the number of individuals we reached; ultimately we tracked the value of the program as measured through specific interventions that could be traced back to individual or team participation in a workshop or roadshow.

I want to add that for me personally the ultimate satisfaction came from the comments attendees put on the surveys. Some senior executives asserted that everyone in the company could benefit from the content. But beyond the content, we were offering a rich and meaningful experience with lessons that extended far beyond the professional environment. One person said, "This was the single best day I've had at Wells Fargo in my 14-year tenure here." People started telling us stories about how they were simplifying their entire life! One senior leader shared that she was no longer buying three kinds of dog food, storing four sets of china, or buying three kinds of toilet paper ("The cheap stuff for the kids, the medium quality for me and my husband, and the fancy grade for guests!").

We were fuelled by anecdote after anecdote, business case by business case, and those of us who were working on the program agreed it was maybe the most meaningful work we had ever done.

Business result

The program generated real value. A few highlights:

Our merchant payment processing team (the group that sets up small businesses to take credit card payments) decided to put simplicity at the centre of their customer strategy. Within a year, they reported a decrease in the amount of time it took to fulfil a customer request for a payment processing system by about 10 days; moreover, they shortened the contract from 16 pages to three.

Our treasury management team (payables and receivables for our biggest corporate and institutional customers) named a "Simplicity Czar" and set out to simplify everything from their relationship management routines to their business architecture.

We featured internal examples, too, because we wanted to simplify our internal operations. Interestingly, during the time we were in operation with this program, Siegel and Gale released their study, "Simplicity at Work", that proved definitively something we had already theorized: that customer experience was directly influenced by employee experience. In other words, if your employees are facing complexity every day, this will, with certainty, end up being reflected in the customer experience.

One internal example stands out. We asked our Head of Benefits if we could feature their annual "open enrollment" email in the program. We thought it would be a perfect object lesson, because it was a dense sea of text with all kinds of directions, footnotes, and way, way too much detail when the sole purpose of the email was to get people to click through and engage with their benefit choices in some way. Their only metric was how many people clicked through. That's what mattered. This enlightened leader agreed to let us use the email as an example of an employee experience that was overly complex and could benefit from simplification if we came back to her with ideas the attendees had generated. We did. We synthesized dozens of ideas and delivered them to her team. The following year the click-through rate increased by over 60%. Team members really responded favourably to the simplified language, clear call to action, and thoughtful use of icons and imagery.

Sustaining a movement

The program had incredible momentum after about two years. The demand was high. I should mention that this project was not a full-time job for the three principals supporting it; and even though we were like a well-oiled machine, running workshops, delivering roadshows, and tracking and reporting results, there came a time when we realized we needed help if we were to sustain the program.

Before I explain that, let me explain how we divided the work. I was in charge of content and delivery. I was the primary content strategist, deciding what was in or out, and I was the main facilitator. My colleague Lucas Freed acted in sort of a business development role. He generated interest throughout all areas of the company and was the initial intake contact for any group seeking participation. I found myself saying many times that without Lucas we would not have been successful. Every good idea needs a master promoter. He was passionate, tireless and fearless. He believed in the program as much as anyone and would espouse its benefits whenever he could. Finally, we had a "producer" who handled tactics, but each person who served in that role over the three or four years' tenure of the program ended up contributing to content and facilitation as well. Kristin Saunders was our first, and when she was promoted in her job she handed the reins to Marise Phillips, who in turn hired Nancy Jonathans to help and then lead that function.

Still, we needed more help, and that's when we landed on the idea of enlisting the community of impassioned workshop alumni – team members who had gone through the course and expressed a desire to help in some way. We started by sending an email to roughly 400 team members explaining that we were starting a Simplicity Fellows program and, with the permission of their managers, we could use their help from 4 to 8 hours a month. We invited them to a call where we explained the program and presented a structure that divided all the tasks we needed done across six "majors": content, facilitation, logistics, visual design, business development, and tech support (we had a robust website at the point with hundreds of inspiring examples and tools). Of the 400 people we approached, more than 90 came to the kick-off call, and of those about 45 agreed to help, taking on tasks or leadership of the various workstreams. It really says something about a corporate program when you get busy people stepping up to carve out time to help advance it.

Evolving

Honestly I could have continued doing that project for many years more, but we decided to roll the simplicity message and techniques into a broader "innovation fundamentals" program, in progress at the time of writing.

This program changed me professionally in profound ways. It shifted my priorities and allowed me to view customers and team members with considerably more empathy and a true belief that simplicity principles are the antidote for our most complex principles. I will add that during this time in my life, I became a yoga teacher as a side-gig and to follow another passion of mine. I'm continually amazed at the overlap between simplicity as a business strategy and the wisdom of the yogic masters going back thousands of years who believe that finding happiness means living simply and removing our grasp on things that don't really matter.

Notes
1. https://www.ted.com/talks/alansiegelletssimplifylegaljargon
2. https://psycnet.apa.org/record/2000-16701-012
3. https://www.siegelgale.com/new-siegelgale-study-shows-simple-work-places-foster-employee-engagement/

Conclusion
Design is the game that matters

WITH THE OUTBREAK of the Covid-19 pandemic, "virtual" has become the new norm. Some companies are now forced to make the change. The speed of digital transformation has been accelerated to the degree we actually feel it. People's fitness routines have changed to virtual studios, school is taking place in virtual classrooms. Recently, some large banks announced that wealth management services would go fully online.[1]

On a positive note, the world has shifted its perspective on how "virtual" is full of possibilities. More than ever, we can now pursue a flexible life working and living anywhere and leveraging networks from all over the world without the barriers of geographic location. We see the possibilities and benefits of working from home; experts estimate that after the pandemic, the work-from-home model will continue to be pervasive.[2]

On the other hand, in the midst of the new normal, we long for rich human interaction. We begin to realise that nothing can replace this in the way we learn, collaborate and run businesses. When the pandemic crisis eases, a new era will begin, one in which we design for optimised human experience. **For after having experienced the possibility of a virtual world, we are now in a better place than ever to design experiences that intersect digital technology and humanity.** And in that intersection of digital technology and humanity lies simplicity.

I do hope you can start this journey with an optimistic heart, with the principles and methods I have shared in this book. If you didn't have time to read the whole book, perhaps the key takeaways below can simplify your reading experience:

- **Simplicity is an experience that makes things easier for users and leaves positive emotions.** Simplicity is a human desire, and the constant force of innovation. Achieving simplicity requires everyone's awareness, mindsets and skills.

- **Get fuelled by empathy.** Empathising with your customers is worth the effort, because it has a direct connection to your ability to reframe – giving you a new lens to look at your innovation challenge.

- **Dance with complexity.** Your stakeholders are your dance partners; learning to mobilise them to tackle complexity is key to success. Change happens only when individuals change.

- **Focus.** Find the North Star of your innovation endeavour in the overlap between customers "jobs", and your business's "why". Competitive advantage lies in doing fewer but better things fabulously.

- **Speak human.** In the digital world, your words are the new interface for engaging customers. Humanise your communication at all touchpoints, from marketing materials to forms and legal documents.

- **Design lovable experiences.** The goal of simplicity is to leave a positive emotional effect, whether it is confidence, pleasure or love. Embrace the value of aesthetics and heighten your sensitivity to design your customer experience with thoughtful intention, craft and beauty.

Simplicity
Index Cards

HERE ARE 45 BITE-SIZE concepts and tools for practitioners, grouped according to the principles of the Simplicity Diamond.

Throughout my simplicity journey, I developed a set of index cards for my own use – a habit I picked up as a young student. My index cards consisted of quotes, methods and frameworks. Whenever I needed inspiration, or wanted to try a new method, I turned to my index cards. They are such a brilliant way of acquiring and applying knowledge. Perhaps it's the tangibility – the touch of the cards and the proud feeling you get when the deck increases in volume. It's also because of the flexibility. You can pick one card to try, change the order, and create new cards as you experiment and learn.

While achieving simplicity requires applying more than one method as well as lots of practice and perseverance, I hope this set of index cards will help you get started, try out what works best for you, and eventually make our own playbook.

Get fuelled by empathy

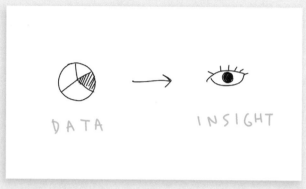

1. Shift your mindset from gathering data to relentlessly seeking insight. (Page 39)

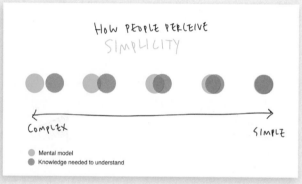

2. Simplicity starts with understanding people. (Page 41)

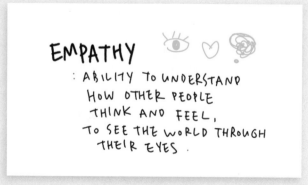

3. Empathy is a strategic asset. (Page 41)

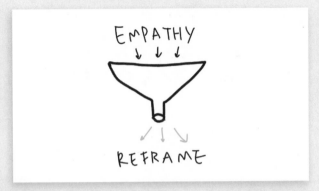

4. There's a direct connection between empathy and the ability to reframe. Invest time in meeting your customers. (Page 42)

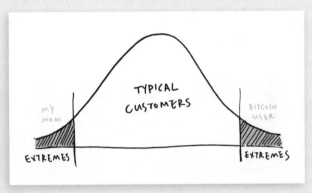

5. Be inspired by extreme users. (Page 51)

6. A customer is a whole person, not a just a consumer. (Page 52)

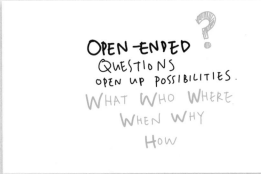

7. Use open-ended questions to collect stories. (Page 52)

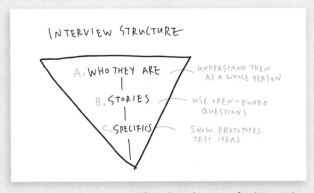

8. Structure your interview from broad to specific. (Page 54)

9. Distinguish data from insight. What customers say is merely data; we need to uncover insights from that. (Page 65)

10. Research doesn't end at collecting data. Synthesise to craft powerful insights. (Page 67)

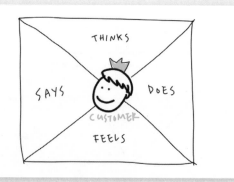

11. Opportunities can be found where what your customers say differs from what they actually do or feel. (Page 71)

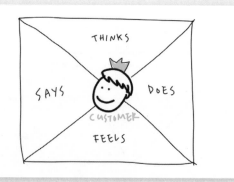

12. To reframe, look for contrasts between your assumptions and what you discovered about customers' behaviour. (Page 75)

Dance with complexity

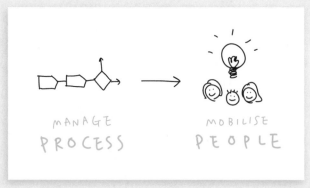

13. Dealing with complexity is about people. Shift your perspective from managing processes to mobilising people. (Page 77)

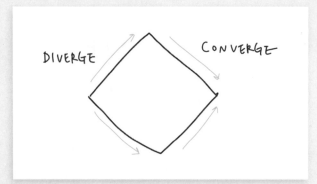

14. Any innovation project is essentially change management. Change happens when people change. (Page 83)

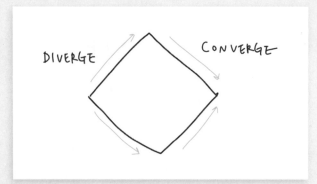

15. Unlock creativity through a structured approach of divergent and convergent thinking. (Page 85)

16. It's a better strategy to create different boxes to think with, rather than thinking "out of the box". (Page 86)

17. The size of the box needs to be "just right" to harness group creativity. (Page 87)

18. Co-create with stakeholders. When people co-create, they become part of the story. (Page 88)

19. Develop your visual vocabulary. Visualising complexity helps people understand and clarify. (Page 96)

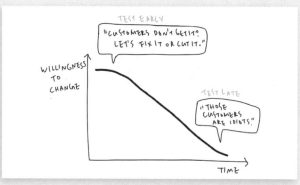

20. The willingness to change is higher when we test earlier. (Page 105)

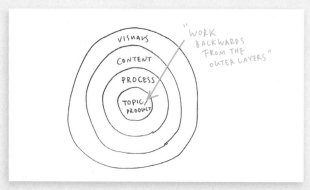

21. Prototype the visible layers to tackle deeper layers of complexity. (Page 107)

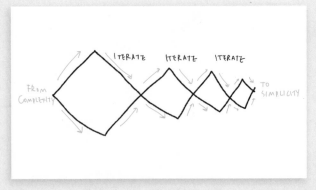

22. Only through an iterative divergent-convergent process, complexity strips off. (Page 111)

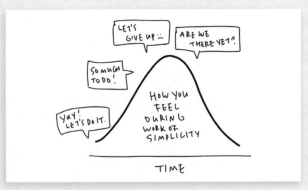

23. It's normal to feel this way during the simplification process. Keep going. (Page 113)

24. The more pain you soak up, the simpler your customers' experience will be. (Page 115)

Focus

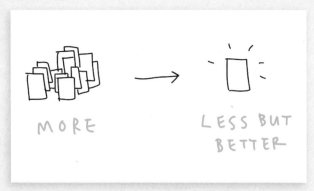

25. Find your innovation opportunities in doing fewer things but better. (Page 117)

26. Focus is an asset. Start with a no-device policy to safeguard your team's focus. (Page 117)

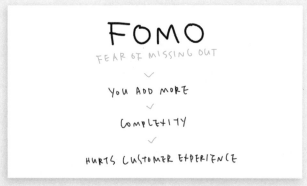

27. FOMO (Fear of missing out) creates complexity. (Page 119)

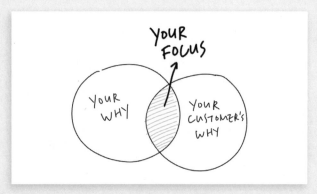

28. Your focus lies between your why and your customers' why. (Page 122)

29. Focus on helping customers get their jobs done well. (Page 127)

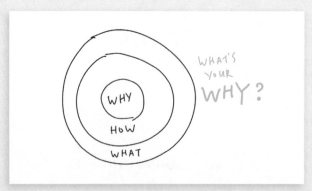

30. Articulating your why drives focused innovation. (Page 129)

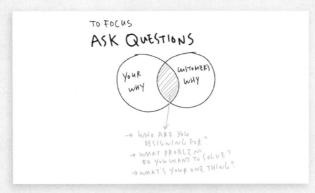

31. Ask yourself these questions to identify the sweet spot – where you can create the most value. (Page 135)

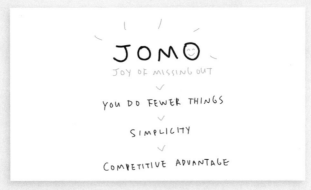

32. Once all questions are answered, articulate your focus using this statement. (Page 137)

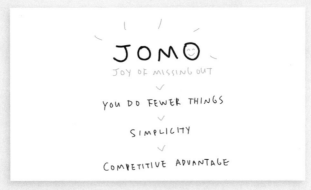

33. Focus means doing fewer things fabulously. Find joy in missing out. (Page 139)

Speak human

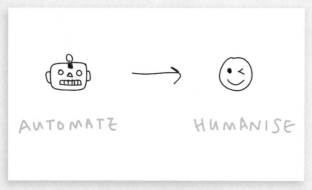

34. Shift your mindset from automation to humanising experiences. (Page 141)

35. The elements of human conversation are the secret to simplifying complex communications of all kinds. (Page 145)

36. We are wired to digest stories to make sense and to be inspired. Use stories to simplify communications. (Page 157)

Design lovable experiences

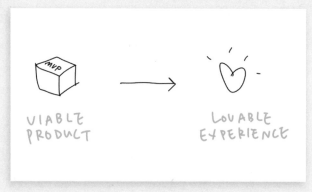

37. Go beyond making just a viable product to crafting lovable experiences. (Page 177)

38. Simplicity is not leaving things at bare minimum. It's an experience that leaves a positive emotion. (Page 177)

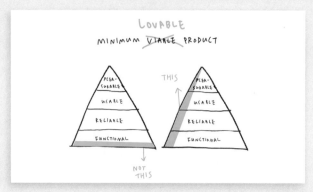

39. Don't stop at Minimum Viable Product. Embrace the full spectrum of user needs to make a lovable experience. (Page 182)

40. Journey mapping allows us to see the big picture and understand users' experiences in great detail. (Page 184)

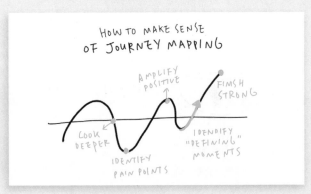

41. Don't dwell only on pain points. There are many ways to make sense of journey mapping. (Page 190)

42. Look for moments to create a memorable experience. Micro moments are useful in designing digital products. (Page 194)

43. Even if you are designing a digital product, do look for opportunities to design the whole experience. (Page 198)

44. Aesthetics are becoming more critical to success, as they are related to how people feel about your products. (Page 200)

LEARN
VISUAL DESIGN

CONTRAST
FLOW
VISUAL HIERARCHY
WHITE SPACE

45. Heighten your design sensitivity and learn the basic rules of visual design. (Page 205)

Notes

"THE MOST PERSONAL IS THE MOST CREATIVE," said director Bong Joon-ho on accepting the Best Director Oscar for *Parasite*, referencing advice that he had received from Martin Scorsese. My sources of inspiration are primarily drawn from my project work, my personal observations and lessons learned, rather than showcasing other great examples from world-famous companies. It's because I wanted to share the depth of the simplification process in which I was personally involved, tried, failed and learned. As a Korean designer who has worked in Switzerland and Singapore, I have developed my own unique perspectives, and I have come to believe that the most personal is indeed the most creative.

My sources for the simplification methods stem from human-centred design, also known as Design Thinking. I personally prefer the term human-centred design as it connotes the intent of the process – putting people at the centre of what we do. In hindsight, it makes logical sense to look to human-centred design to simplify, because simplicity is based on human nature and it's about getting closer to people's mental models.

These days, companies look to use the "problem-solving process" side of design as an innovation method, which is the right thing to do. But instead of using design exclusively as a process, I also wanted to emphasise the *craft* side of design – the look and feel of things, which I refer to as aesthetics in this book. The craft side of design is what materialises all the problem-solving steps and creates the real visible impact.

Chapter 1

1. Alan Siegel and Irene Etzkorn. (2013). *Simple: Conquering the Crisis of Complexity* (1st ed.). UK: Random House Books.
2. Interview with Mark McCormick by author, March 2017
3. Jérôme Gautier. (2011). *Chanel: The Vocabulary of Style.* Yale University Press.
4. B.J. Fogg. (2019). *Tiny Habits: The Small Changes that Change Everything* (1st ed.). Boston, USA: Houghton Mifflin Harcourt.
5. The World's Simplest Brands 2018–2019, Siegel + Gale. http://simplicityindex.com
6. Richard Koch and Greg Lockwood. (2016). *Simplify: How the Best Businesses in the World Succeed* (1st ed.). UK: Entrepreneur Press.

Chapter 2

1. Ken Segall. (2012). *Insanely Simple: The Obsession that Drives Apple's Success.* NY: Penguin Group.

Chapter 3

1. FRANK by OCBC is a financial services brand targeted at millennials launched in Singapore in 2011. It is a sub-brand of OCBC Bank, a realisation of the bank's strategy to grow the future banking population. As of the time of writing, FRANK by OCBC is the market leader in the millennial segment in Singapore, as the brand continuously evolves to grow to adapt to the needs of dynamic young adults, with a strong digital banking presence as well as active engagement.
2. Scott D. Anthony. (2012). *The Little Black Book of Innovation: How It Works, How to Do It.* Boston: Harvard Business Review Press.
3. "Jeff Bezos banned PowerPoint in meetings. His replacement is brilliant." https://www.inc.com/carmine-gallo/jeff-bezos-bans-powerpoint-in-meetings-his-replacement-is-brilliant.html
4. "Why you only need to test with 5 users." https://www.nngroup.com/articles/why-you-only-need-to-test-with-5-users/ Mar 18, 2000.
5. "Why did Shoes of Prey fail?" https://www.smartcompany.com.au/industries/retail/ shoes-of-prey-listened-customers/ Mar 18, 2019.
6. "The Shoes of Prey journey ends." https://medium.com/@mmmichaelfox/the-shoes-of-prey-journey-ends-34634925f1f, March 11, 2019.
7. Jon Kolko. (2011). *Exposing the Magic of Design* (1st ed.). Oxford University Press.
8. Framing assumptions adapted from Lean Startup Machine Validation Board. https://www.lean- startupmachine.com/validationboard/

Chapter 4

1. John Maeda. (2006). *The Laws of Simplicity*. Cambridge, MA: MIT Press Books.
2. GoBear 2020 Fact Sheet. https://gbdocs.gobear.com/corp/gobear-factsheet.pdf
3. Alan Moore. (2016). *Do Design: Why Beauty is Key to Everything*. New York: The Do Book Company.
4. Adapted from Wikipedia, accessed on Mar 1, 2020.
5. John Zeratsky and Braden Kowitz. (2016). *Sprint: How to Solve Big Problems and Test Ideas in Just Five Days* (1st ed.). UK: Penguin Random House.

Chapter 5

1. Rolf Dobelli. (2017). *The Art of the Good Life* (1st ed.). UK: Sceptre.
2. Wikipedia, accessed on March 11, 2020. https://en.wikipedia.org/wiki/Fear_of_missing_out
3. Barry Schwartz. (2009). *The Paradox of Choice: Why More Is Less*. NY: HarperCollins e-books.
4. Edward De Bono. (1999). *Simplicity*. London: Penguin Books
5. Warren Berger. (2018). *The Book of Beautiful Questions: The Powerful Questions That Will Help You Decide, Create, Connect, and Lead*. NY: Bloomsbury Publishing
6. Harvard Business Review interview with Clayton Christensen on Jobs To Be Done HBR IdeaCast, 2016.
7. Simon Sinek, "How great leaders inspire action." https://www.ted.com/talks/ simonsinekhowgreatleadersinspireaction
8. Joanne's story on FRANKbyOCBC.com and https://www.youtube.com/watch?v=LODo40e2-M
9. Focus statement adapted from elevator pitch by Geoffrey A. Moore, (2014), *Crossing the Chasm* (3rd ed.), Harper Business.

Chapter 6

1. Willian K. Zinsser. (2006). *On Writing Well: The Classic Guide to Writing Nonfiction* (7th ed.). HarperCollins e-books.
2. Annette Simmons. (2019). *The Story Factor: Inspiration, Influence and Persuasion through the Art of Storytelling* (3rd ed.). New York: Hachette Book Group.
3. Structure of story adapted from Donna Lichaw (2016), *The User's Journey: Storymapping Products That People Love*. Brooklyn, NY: Rosenfeld Media, LLC.
4. "What is a brand persona, and do I need one?" https://www.weebly.com/inspiration/brand-persona/, March 13, 2017.

Chapter 7

1. Abraham Maslow. (1943). "A theory of human motivation." *Psychological Review.*
2. Aarron Walter. (2011). *Design for Emotions.* New York: A Book Apart.
3. Eric Ries. (2011). *The Lean Startup: How Today's Entrepreneurs Use Continuous Innovation to Create Radically Successful Businesses.* New York: Crown Business.
4. Chip Heath and Dan Heath. (2017). *The Power of Moments: Why Certain Experiences Have Extraordinary Impact* (1st ed.). UK: Penguin Random House.
5. Micro moments by Google. https://www.thinkwithgoogle.com/marketing-resources/micro-moments/micro-moments-understand-new-consumer-behavior/
6. Mikael Krogerus and Roman Tschäppeler. (2019). *The Communication Book: 44 Ideas for Better Conversations Every Day.* UK: Penguin Random House.
7. "The Aesthetic – Usability effect." https://www.nngroup.com/articles/aesthetic-usability-effect/ January 29, 2017
8. Pauline Brown. (2019). *Aesthetic Intelligence: How to Boost It and Use It in Business and Beyond* (1st ed.). New York: HarperBusiness.
9. Ellen Lupton and Jennifer Cole Phillips. (2015). *Graphic Design: The New Basics* (2nd ed.). New York: Princeton Architectural Press
10. "Complexity to Simplicity." https://medium.com/@chenxidu/complexity-to-simplicity-ccae63ad5678

Chapter 9

1. Annette Simmons. (2019). *The Story Factor: Inspiration, Influence and Persuasion through the Art of Storytelling* (3rd ed.). New York: Hachette Book Group.

Conclusion

1. "OCBC moves wealth advisory service online." https://www.straitstimes.com/business/banking/ocbc-moves-wealth-advisory-service-online?utm_source=STSmartphone&utm_medium=share&utm_term=2020-06-10+06%3A09%3A31 June 9, 2020.
2. "How to keep working from home after Covid-19." https://www.forbes.com/sites/markcperna/2020/05/01/ how-to-keep-working-from-home-after-covid-19/ May 1, 2020.

Image credits

All sketches and photographs by the author unless otherwise specified.

Page 21: Coco Chanel sketch by Sabina Zwicky

Page 24: Financial needs analysis forms – courtesy of OCBC Bank

Page 41: How people perceive simplicity – concept by Bojan Blecic; sketched by author

Page 44–46: FRANK by OCBC prototypes – photos by author, reproduced with permission of OCBC Bank

Page 60: Experience Labs observer room – courtesy of OCBC Bank

Page 71: Empathy mapping – adapted from https://www.nngroup.com/articles/empathy-mapping/; sketched by author

Page 92: Drawing by Sabina Zwicky, 2007

Page 94–95: Visual facilitation session by author with SMU Academy

Page 100–101: Carton box ATM by Sabina Zwicky, 2011; photos by author

Page 104, 106: Early-stage prototypes – photos by author, reproduced with permission of OCBC Bank

Page 105: Early testing graph – original concept by John Knapp, John Zeratsky and Braden Kowitz (2016), *Sprint: How to Solve Big Problems and Test Ideas in Just Five Days* (UK: Penguin Random House).

Page 109: Policy illustration prototype – courtesy of OCBC Bank.

Page 112: Evolution of prototypes – photos by author; reproduced with permission of OCBC Bank.

Page 126: iPod ad image – Apple Archive.

Page 130–131: FRANK by OCBC – courtesy of OCBC Bank.

Page 133: Joanne's story – FRANKbyOCBC.com and https://www.youtube.com/watch?v=LODo40e2-M

Page 133: FRANK by OCBC 3.0 store – by Leong Huang Zi, courtesy of OCBC Bank Experience Design.

Page 134: FRANK by OCBC pictures by a customer featured on Facebook FRANK by OCBC.

Page 150: Insurance product checklist – courtesy of OCBC Bank.

Page 151: GoBear Brand Guide, Q4 2014.

Page 155: Investment letter before and after – courtesy of OCBC Bank.

Page 157: Structure of story – adapted from Donna Lichaw (2016), *The User's Journey: Storymapping Products That People Love* (Brooklyn, NY: Rosenfeld Media, LLC).

Page 159: Brochure before and after simplification.

Page 179: Hierarchy of needs – adapted from Abraham Maslow (1943), "A Theory of Human Motivation", *Psychological Review*.

Page 179: Hierarchy of user needs – adapted from Aaron Walter (2011), *Design for Emotions* (New York: A Book Apart).

Page 182: Minimum Lovable Product – adapted from Jussi Pasanan's work @jopas on Twitter.

Page 186: Journey mapping example – from workshop with Singapore Workforce Professional Conversion Program participants, 2019.

Page 190–191: Journey mapping example – from Singapore Management University executive classes, 2019.

Page 192: Journey mapping example – from OCBC Bank Master Class, 2019.

Page 194: Sketch based on Micro moments by Google https://www.thinkwithgoogle.com/marketing-resources/micro-moments/micro-moments-understand-new-consumer-behavior/.

Page 207–208: Contrast and flow – created by Kong Ming Jie.

Page 216–220: Prototypes and design of digital wealth management service –courtesy of OCBC Bank.

Page 243: OCBC Great Design Principles – courtesy of OCBC Bank.

Page 244–247: Group Customer Experience office – photos by author; reproduced with permission of OCBC Bank.

Page 250: OCBC Design Sprint framework – courtesy of OCBC Bank.

Page 252: Great Design Journal – designed by Weiming Huang; photo courtesy of OCBC Bank Experience Design.

Acknowledgements

WRITING A BOOK ON SIMPLICITY has definitely been a daring adventure. There is a wealth of books out there that inspired me and guided me through my simplicity journey; I thank those authors and practitioners who enlightened me along the way. And because of their great work, it took courage to write about simplicity. It is easy to say you need to simplify, but it is really hard to walk the talk. Particularly as I promote "Speak human", I must confess that I'm guilty of using business jargon and design jargon in this book! I seek your kind understanding and forgiveness.

At this point of writing the book, I am only left with humility and gratitude. This book would not exist without all the people who worked with me, supported me, guided me and challenged me. First of all, huge thanks to the incredible people I met in OCBC Bank, Credit Suisse and IMS Health, who were the sources of my inspiration. In particular, thanks to Bojan Blecic, who possesses a great wealth of design wisdom, and who always reminded the team to ask "What problem we are trying to solve?" in his cool Italian accent; David McQuillen, who inspired me to use design to simplify the complex world of financial services; Ching Wei Hong, for being the fearless leader; Ching Ching Koh, for her guidance and support; Wyson Lim, for partnering with me on the wealth and simplicity journey; Dennis Tan, for the great partnership; Siew Lee Tan, for her energy and hands-on leadership; Evelyn Yeo, for the awesome project and fun we had; Lim Khiang Tong, for bringing design and IT together; Praveen Raina, for promoting "No more ugliness"; Pranav Seth, for pushing the boundaries; Aye Wee Yap and her team on OCBC campus, who made all the Simplicity Bootcamps run so smoothly; Dawn Lim and Wui Tek Woon, for the great journey we took on the "Speak human" journey; Geneviene Gay, for pouring out all her passion; and Aditya Gupta, for the sharp insights and great digital projects we ran together. And big love and thanks to my Experience Design team (ex-)colleagues, who worked tirelessly to deliver simplicity and who really are the best designers in the world: Natalie Koh, Huang

Zi Leong, Jeremy Ng, Jordan Ng, Weiming Huang, Franklin Wuu, Esmerella Fong, Samuel Poh, Torsten Starcke, Saraphina Ching, Fabian Ng, Yong Hwa Liow, Erene Ng, Ming Jie Kong and Li Li Lim. I thank Rob Findlay for creating a wonderful platform to connect passionate practitioners. I would also like to extend my gratitude to my clients and most supportive partners, particularly Dr Lai Cheng Lim, Michael Low and Sarah Yip at Singapore Management University Academy, my executive students for being so open with me, and all the wonderful people I have worked with.

Huge thanks to my contributors for sharing their wisdom: Mark McCormick, who is the most inspiring strategist and practitioner; Jung-Joo Lee, who brings clarity and depth into design methods; Eric Chin, who is a true change-maker; Tiia Maekinen, who is more passionate about experience design than myself; and Deepa Vijayan, who is not only a great writer, but also helped me give birth to this book! I'm very grateful to my editor, Justin Lau, who appreciates good design, for being so patient with me; my publisher, Melvin Neo, who gave me this wonderful opportunity to write; Rob Ballantine, for reminding me to be myself in writing; and Sze Wei Lee and Jon Jon Muhammad, who spent a lot of time reading my long ugly drafts.

My biggest thanks go to my family. My daughter Sabina, who always inspires me with her creativity and who helped me with artwork in this book. My sister Mi Jeong, who guided me through the writing process, especially when I lost courage to keep going. My brother Yuta, for taking me to Mount Fuji. My mom, who taught me what empathy means. My son Ben, who took care of his younger brother so that I could find time to write this book. My little 4-year-old son Noah, who always gives me loads of kisses. And my husband, Jonas, who has been my stable foundation, always bringing me back to simplicity.

About the author

JIN KANG MØLLER is an award-winning customer experience strategist, designer and management consultant. She was born in Seoul, and raised by parents of the post–Korean War generation. She always found the city's buzz and complexity fascinating, which led her to study Visual Communications and Product Design, perhaps to equip herself to design for simplicity.

Throughout her career, Jin has designed customer experiences for private banking, wealth management, insurance and pharmaceutical businesses, and created bottom-line impact. She has a proven track record of successful execution of her design methodologies in European and Asian markets.

She has held design leadership positions in OCBC Bank in Singapore and Credit Suisse in Switzerland, creating a movement to distil methods and mindsets of human-centred design across the organisation. She was the driving force behind FRANK by OCBC, an award-winning millennial banking concept that positioned the bank as the market leader in the segment. She defined the new digital wealth management concept (launched as the OCBC OneWealth app), which drove successful digital sales and won her a Singapore Good Design Mark (SG Mark) Gold award in 2017. With 20 years' practitioner's experience, Jin is a highly acclaimed trainer and Affiliate Faculty at Singapore Management University Academy, where she teaches executive programmes on innovation, customer experience and design leadership, which have become one of the highest-ranked programmes.

Currently, her focus is on helping organisations develop and scale innovation capabilities through the power of design and simplicity. Having successfully consulted and coached over a thousand executives across industries from financial services and technology to healthcare and government, Jin continues to inspire and empower change-makers in organisations across the world.

She lives in Basel, Switzerland, with her family, and is always looking for ways to design simplicity in life.

Meet Jin at DesignfulCompany.com